Color Puppy Home

Activity & Coloring Book

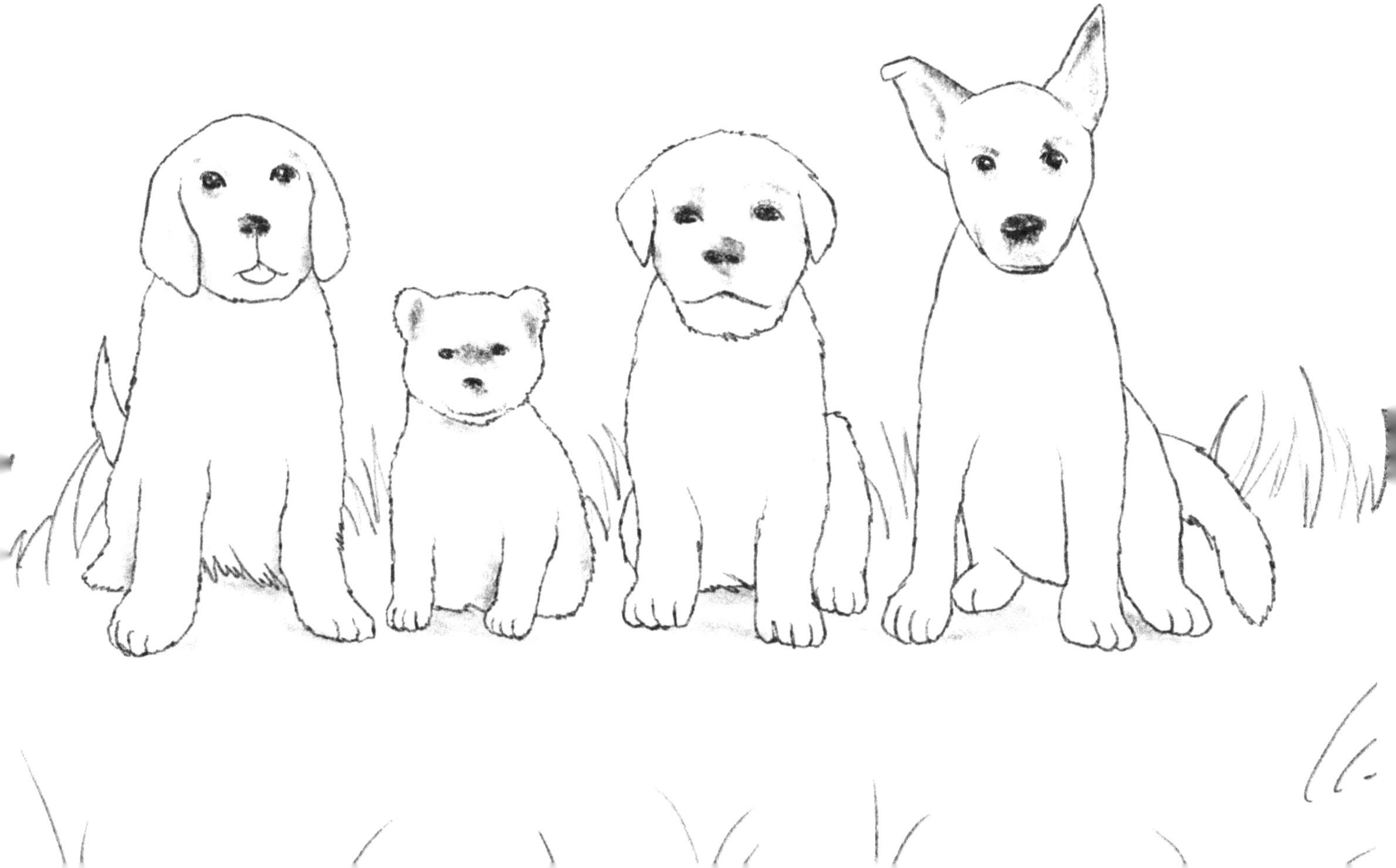

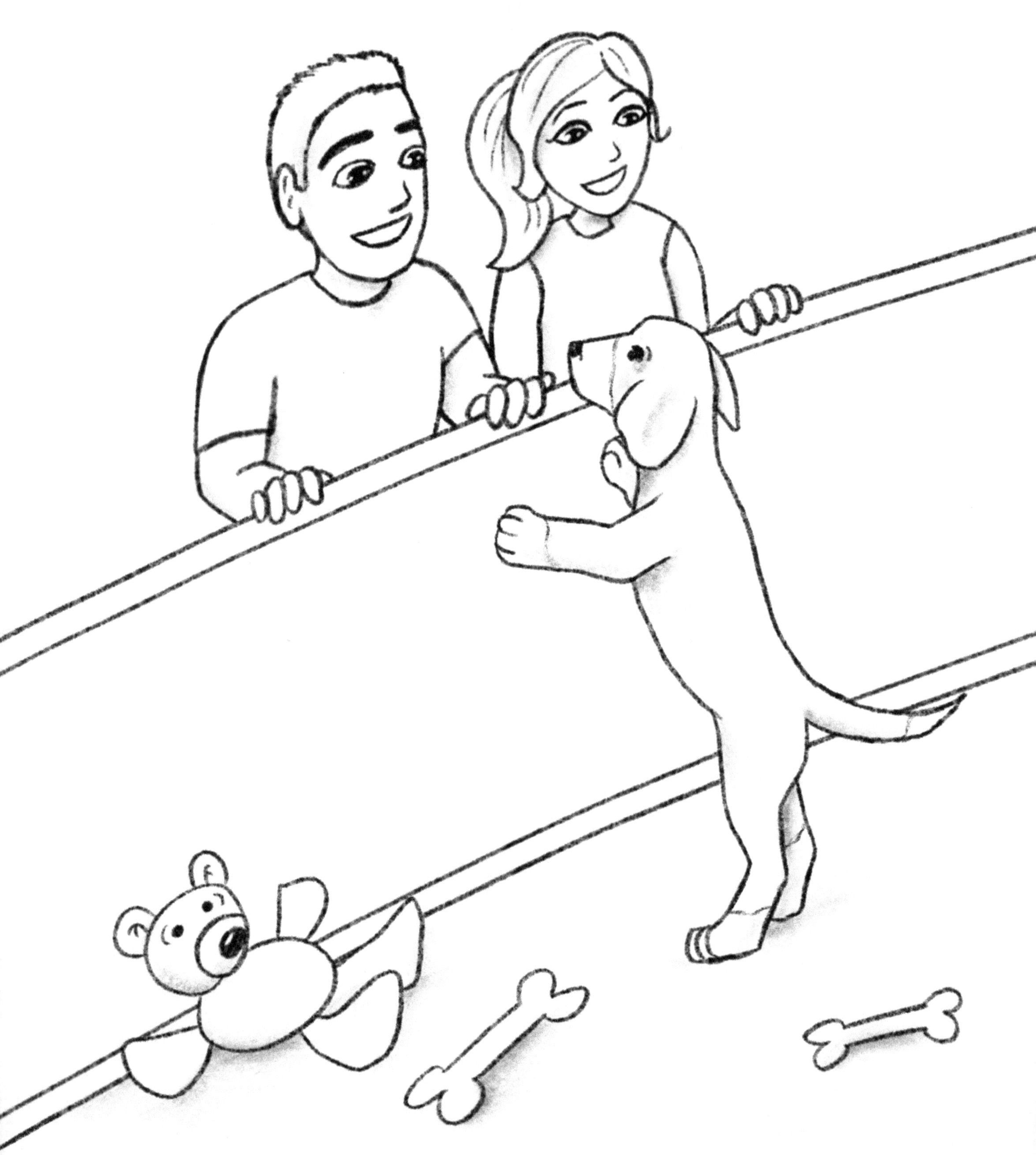

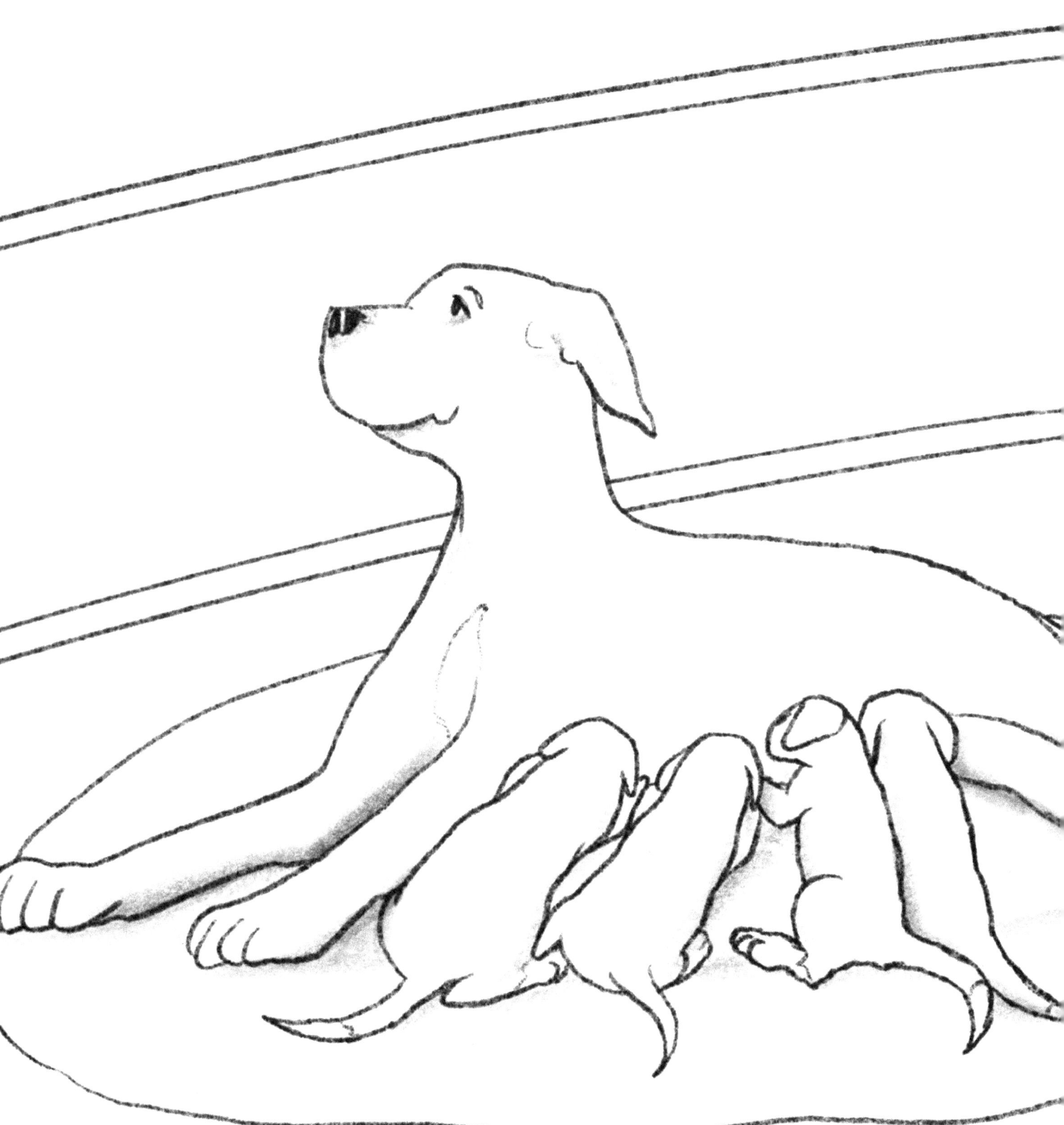

CONNECT THE DOTS AND DRAW YOUR OWN ABBEY!

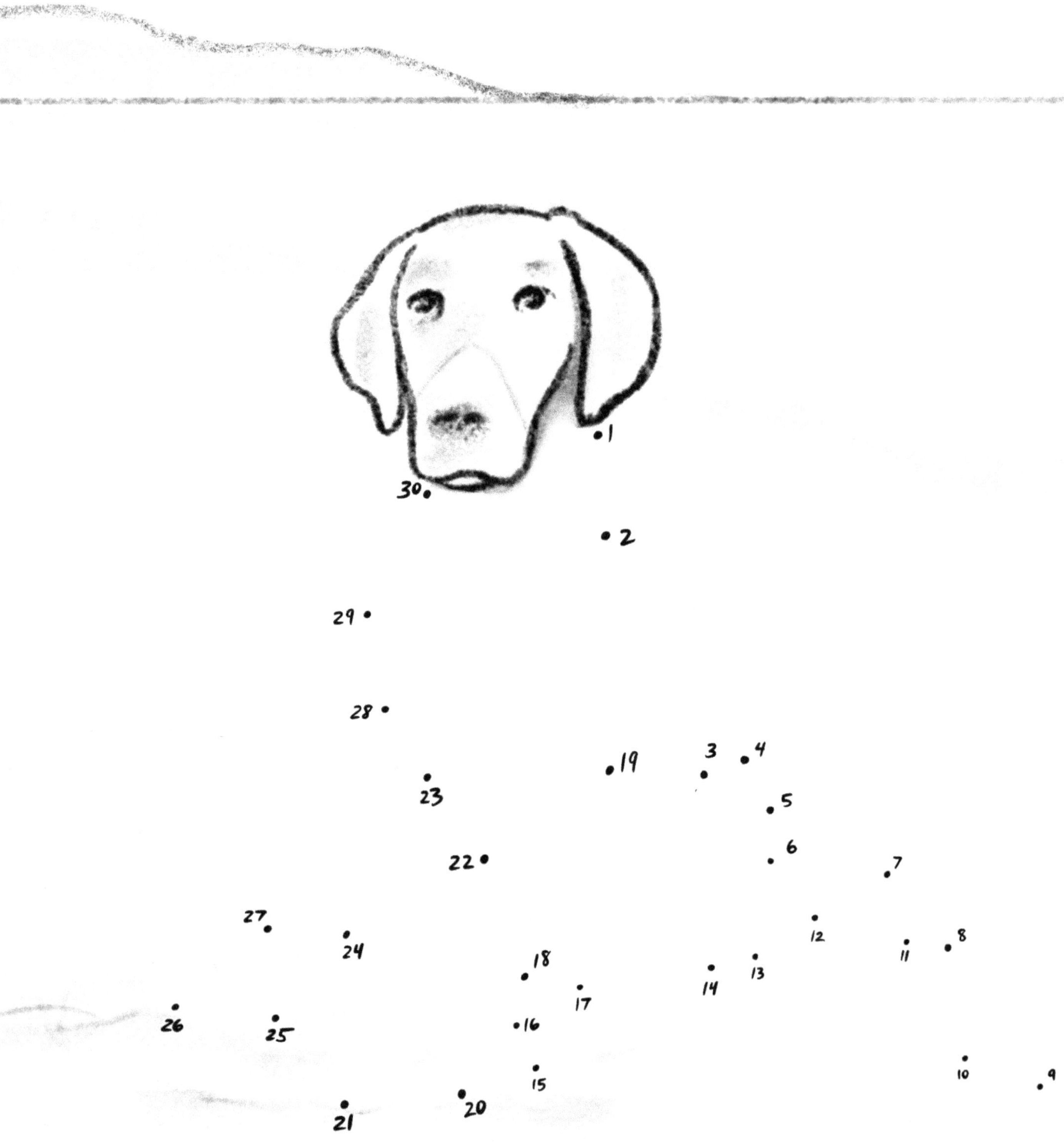

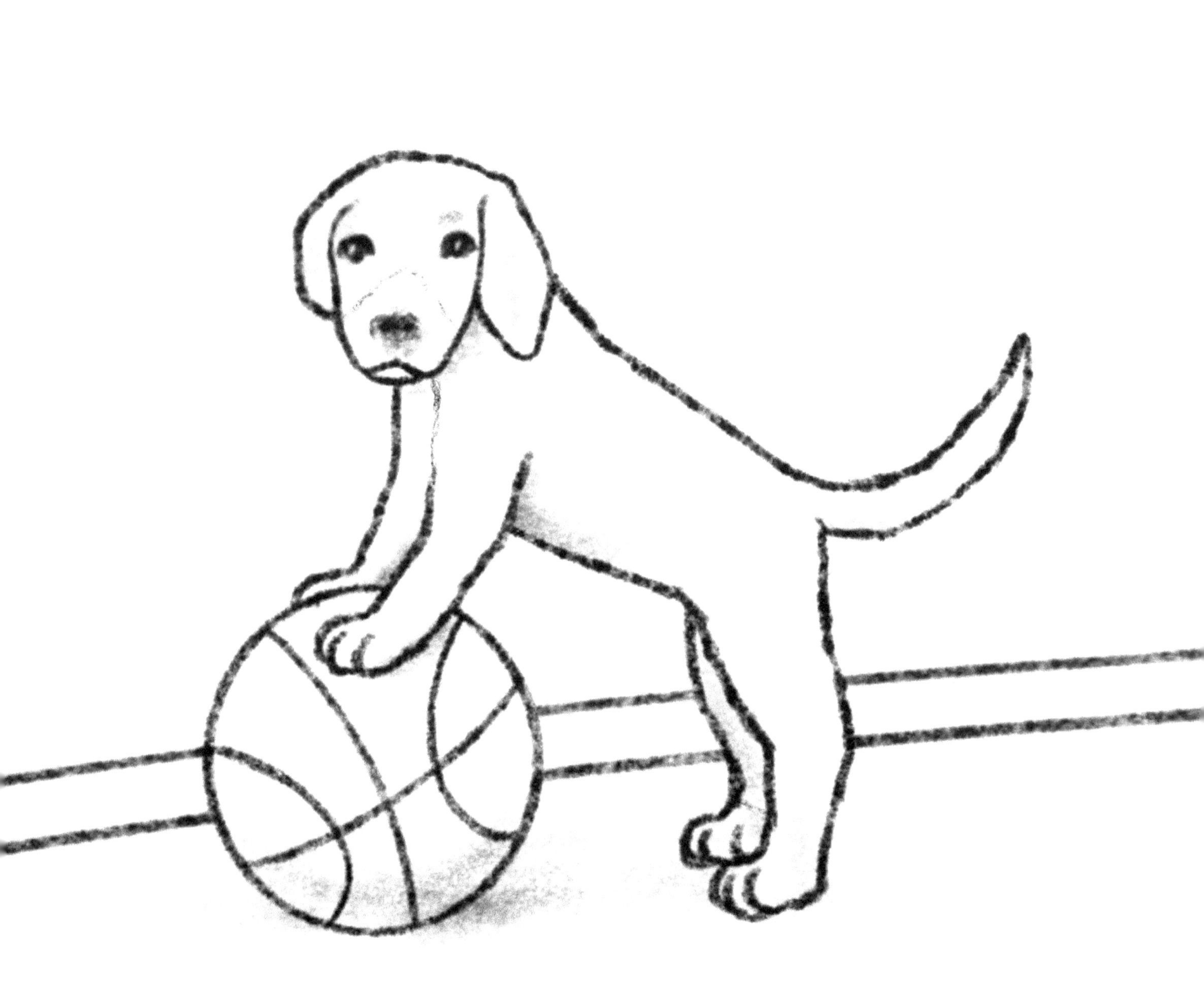

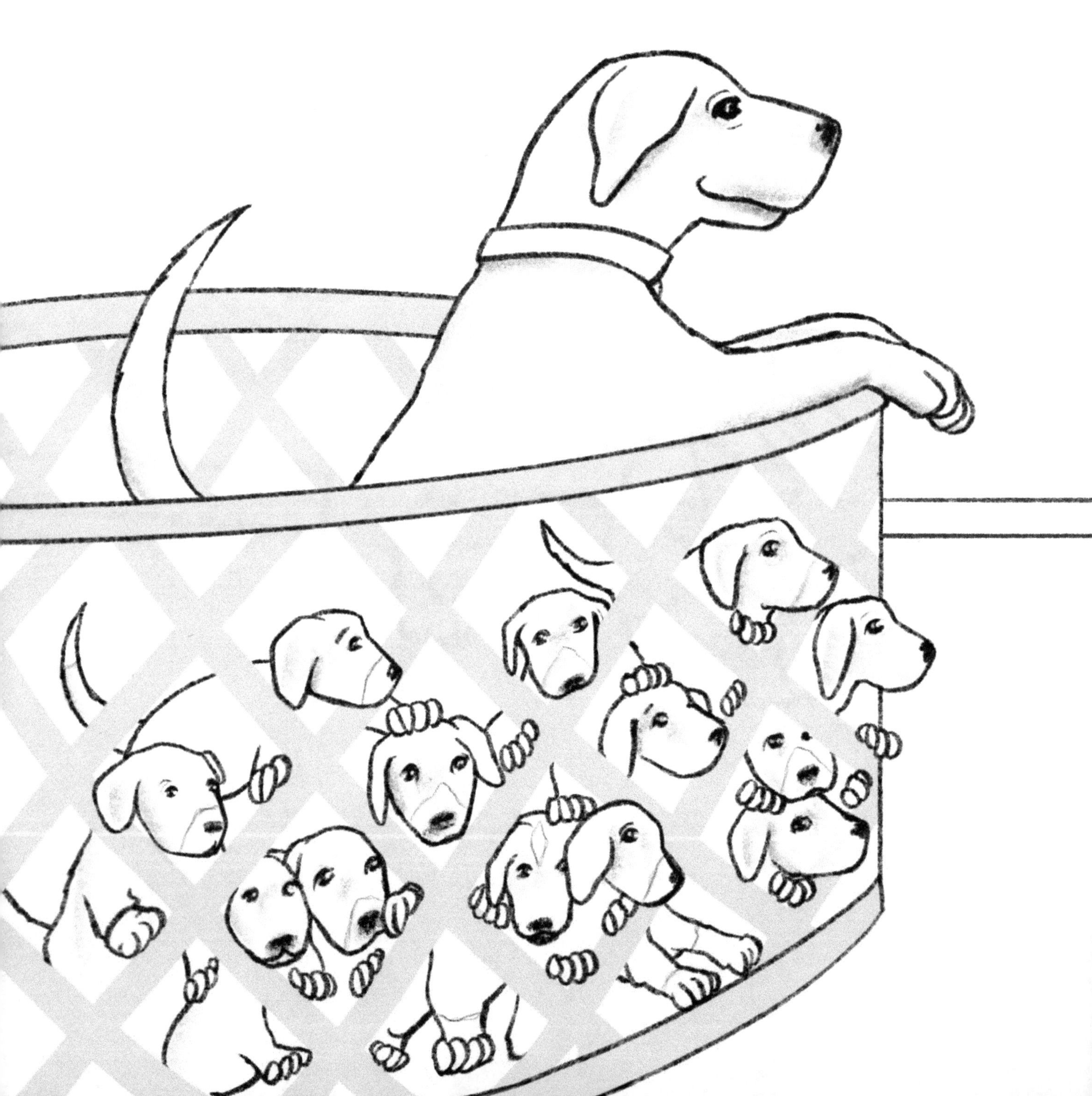

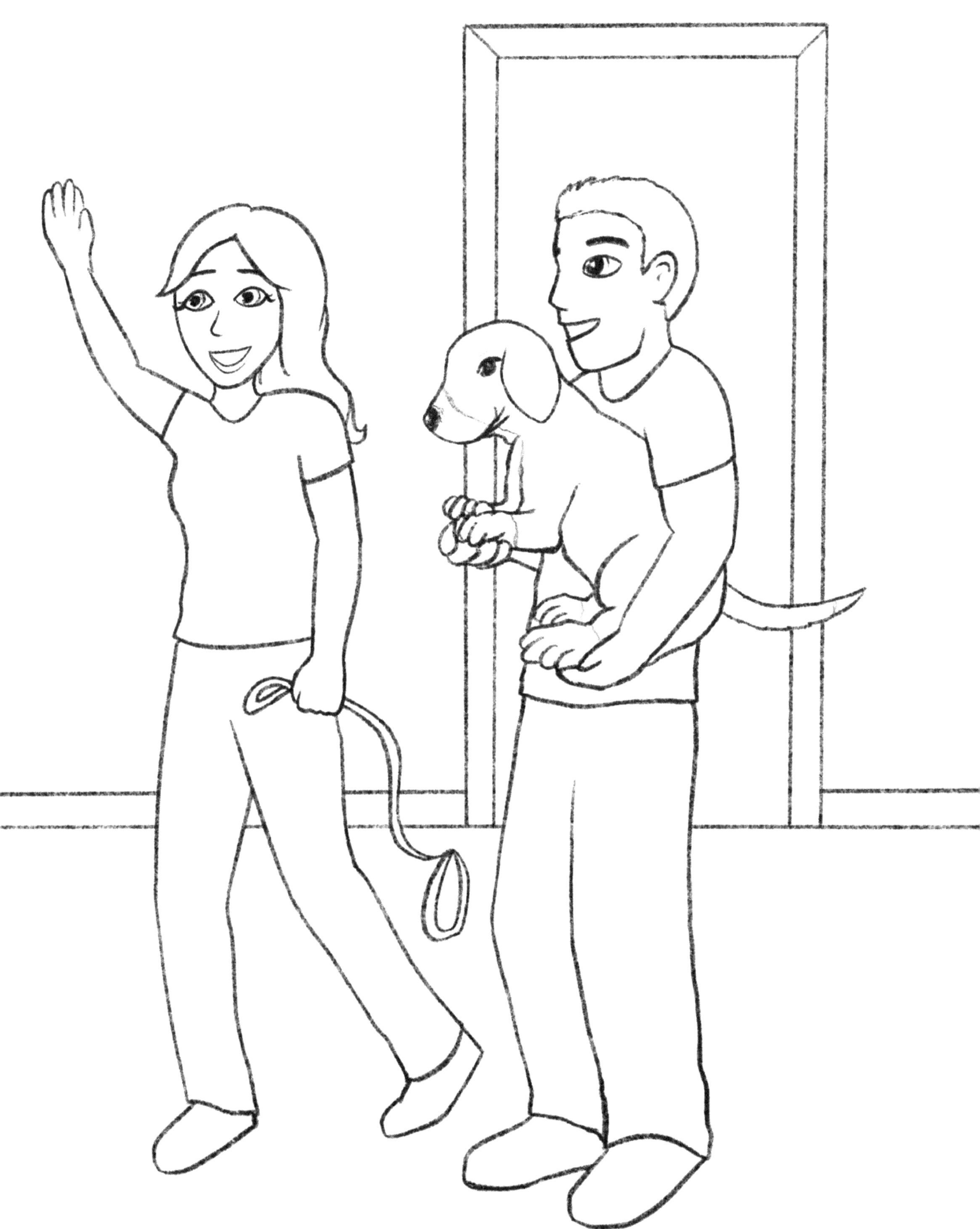

THERE ARE 12 BONES IN THIS PICTURE,
CAN YOU FIND THEM ALL?

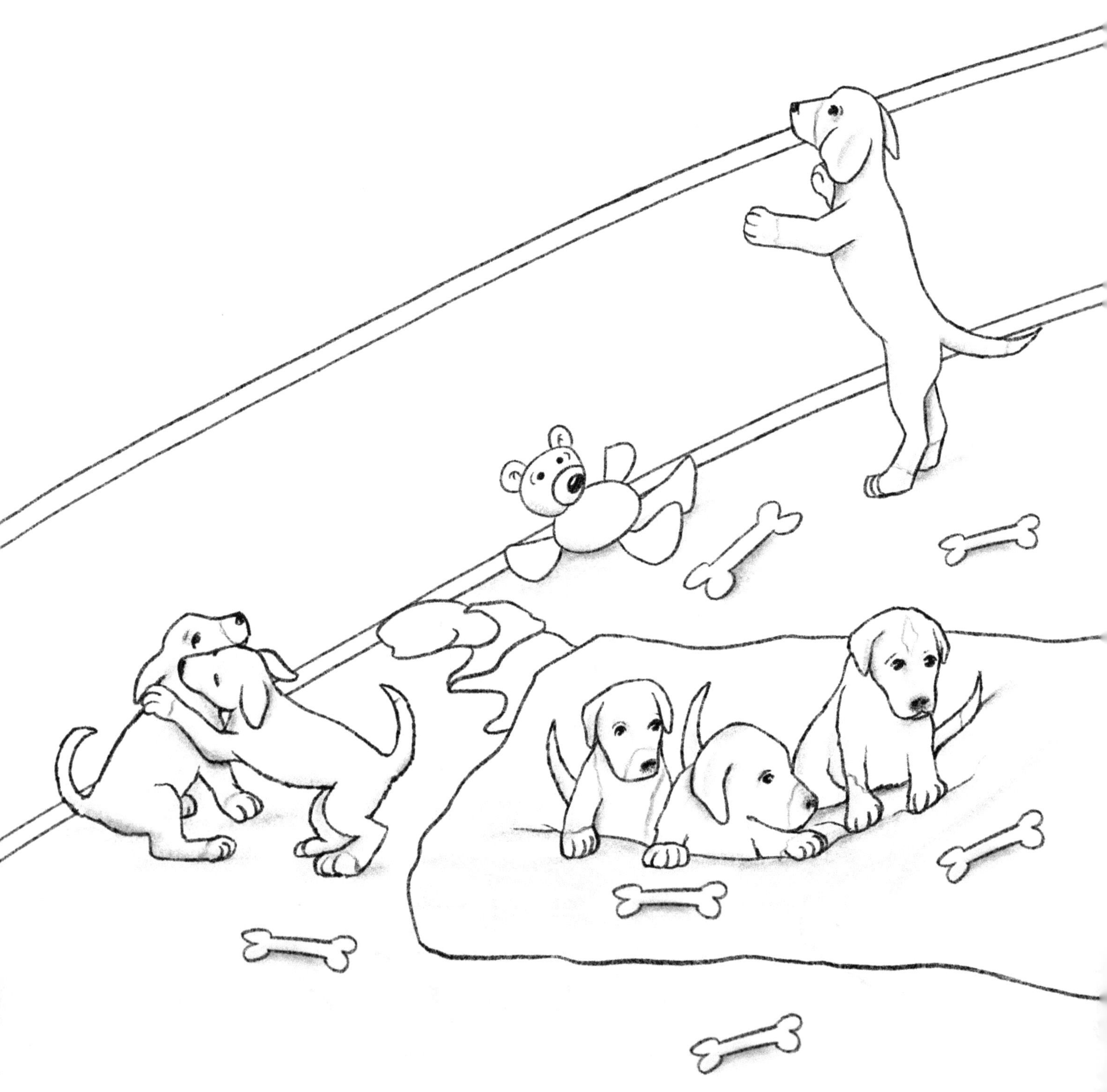

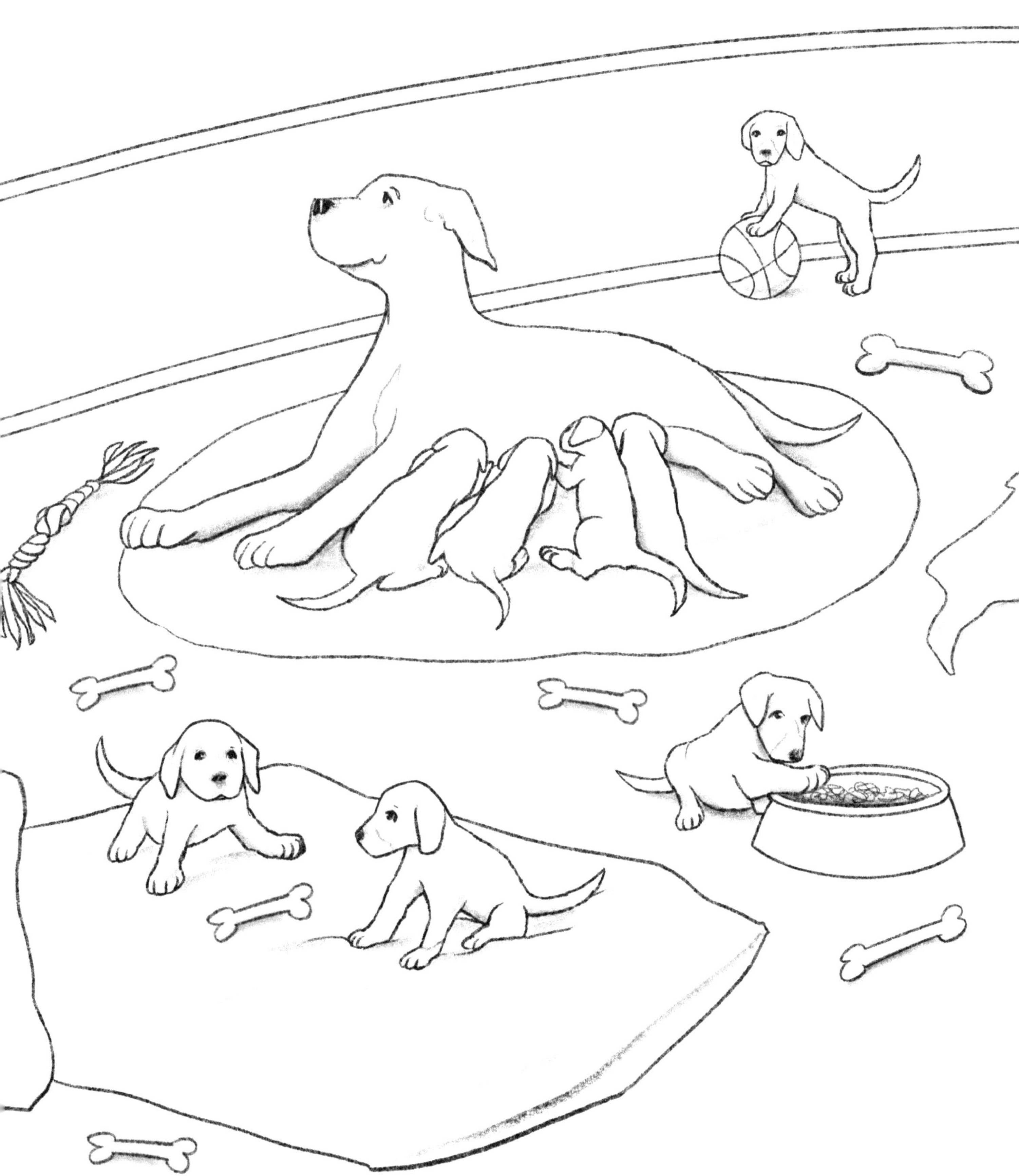

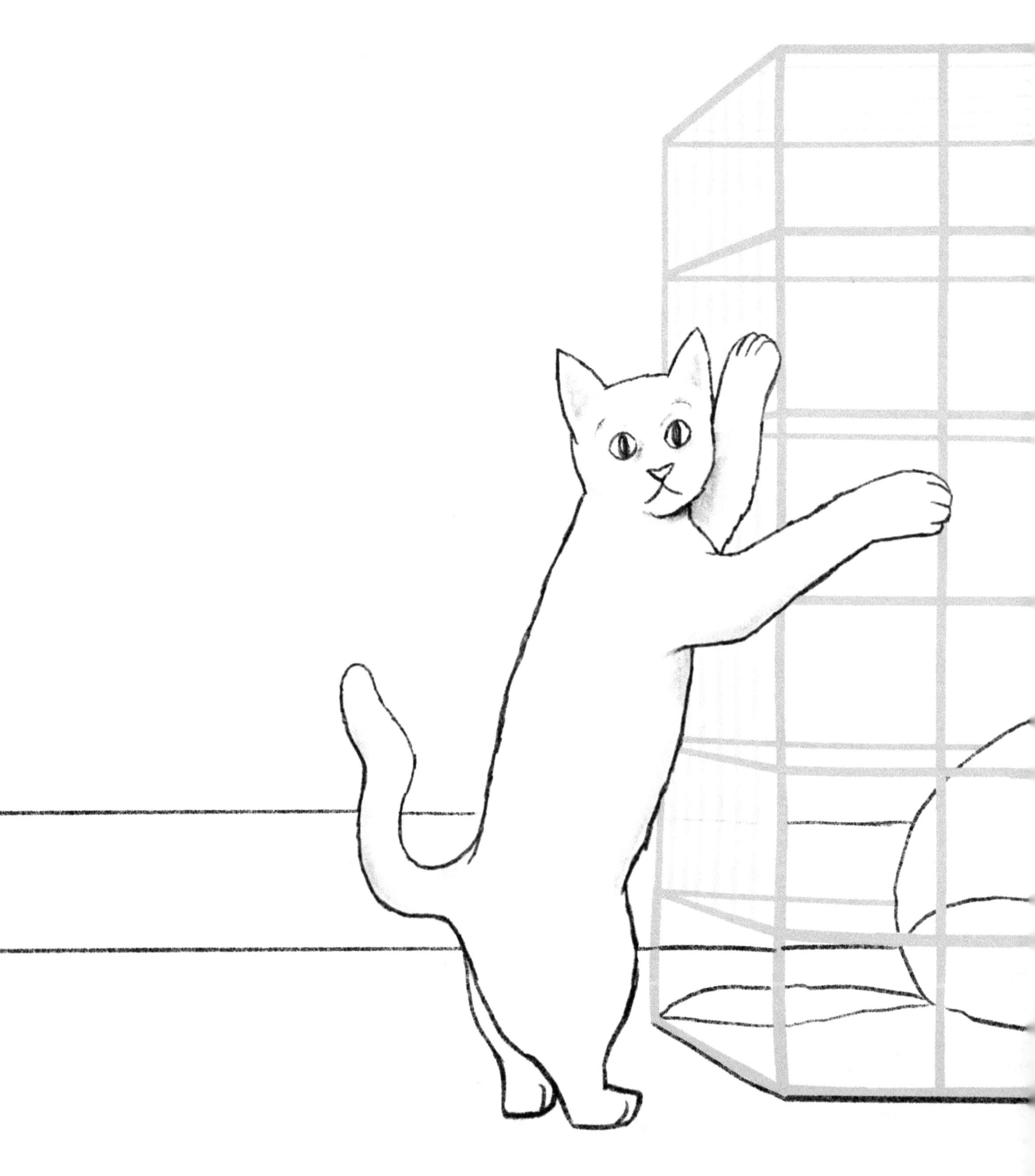

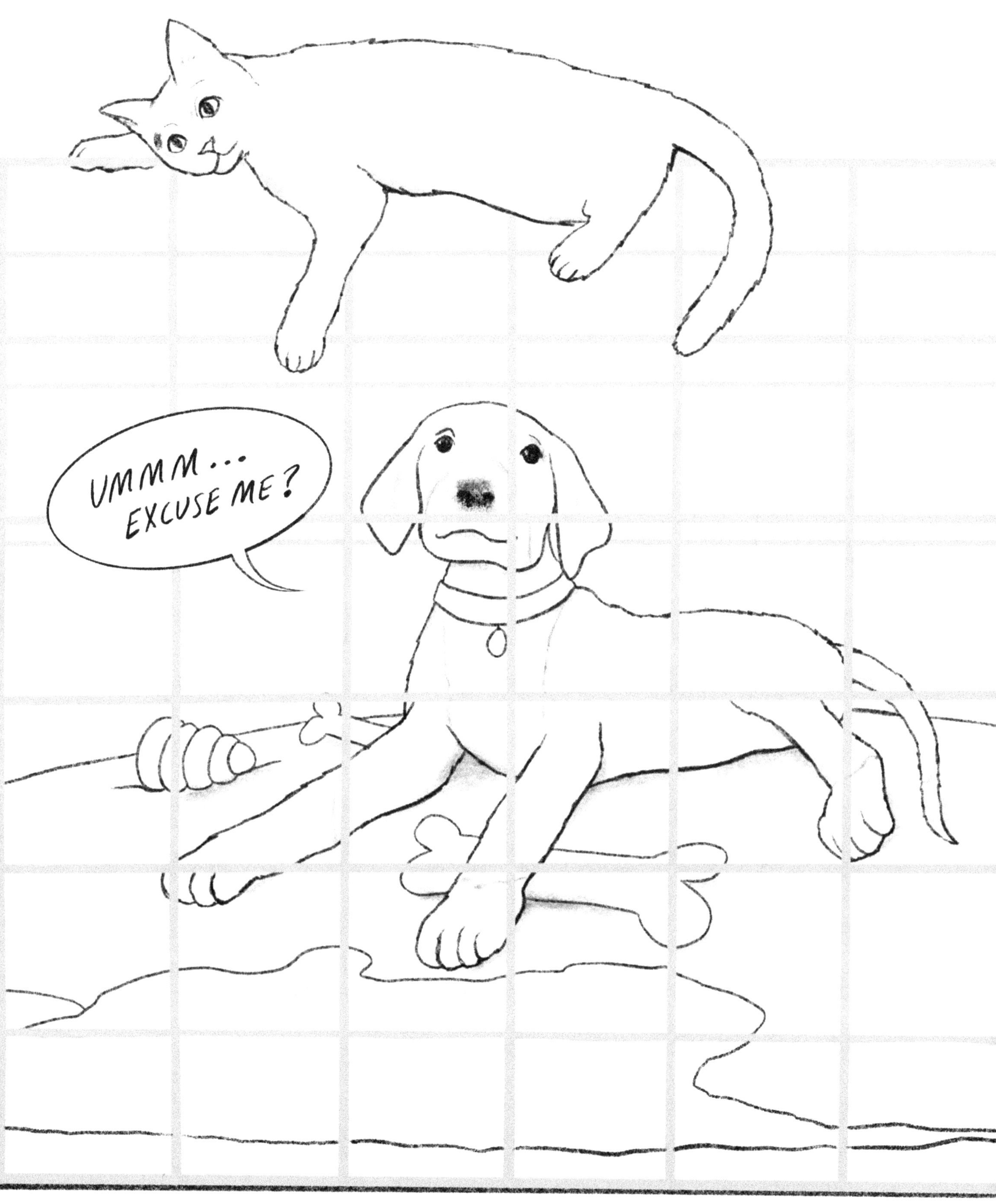
UMMM...
EXCUSE ME?

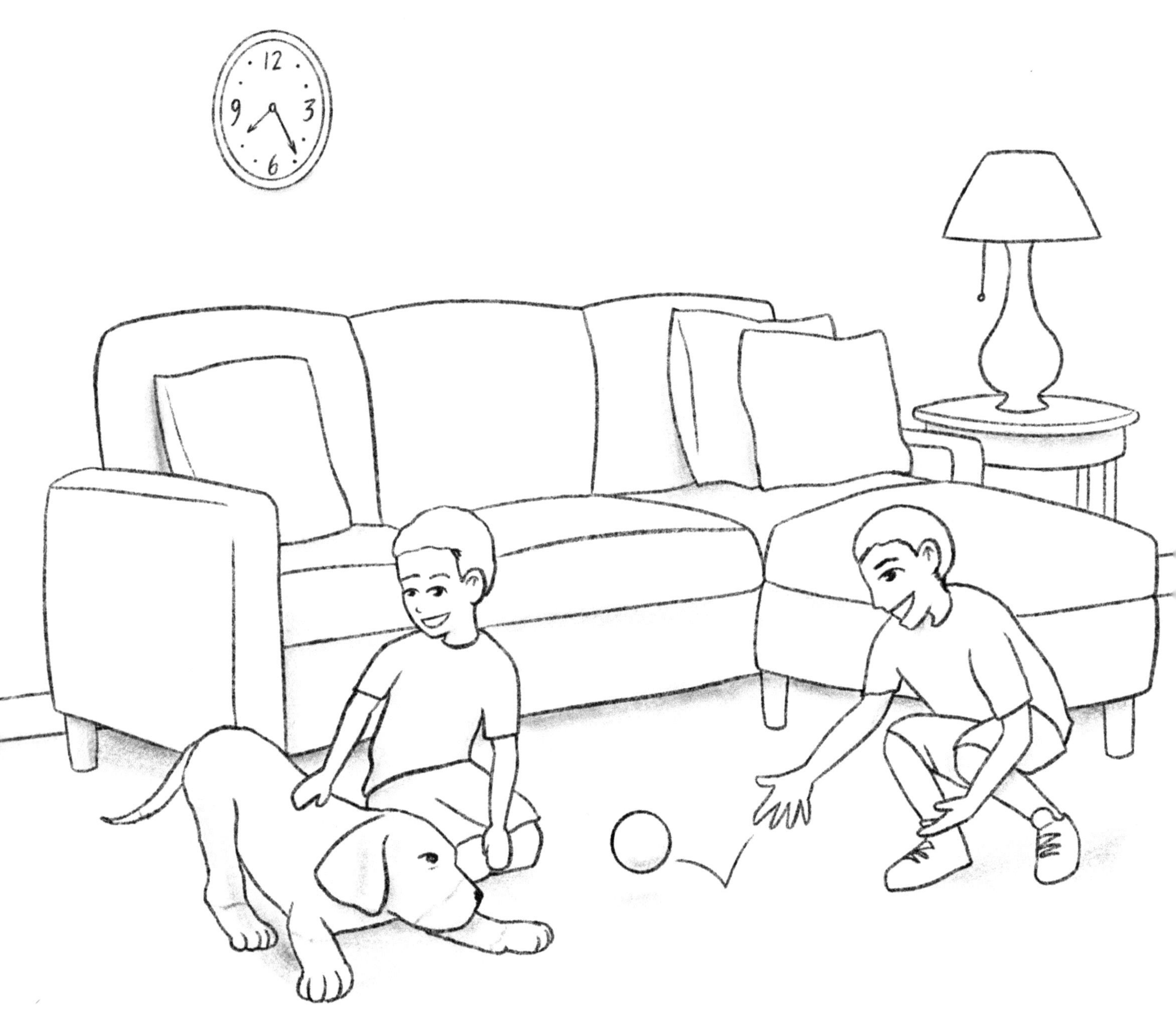

FETCH, ABBEY!

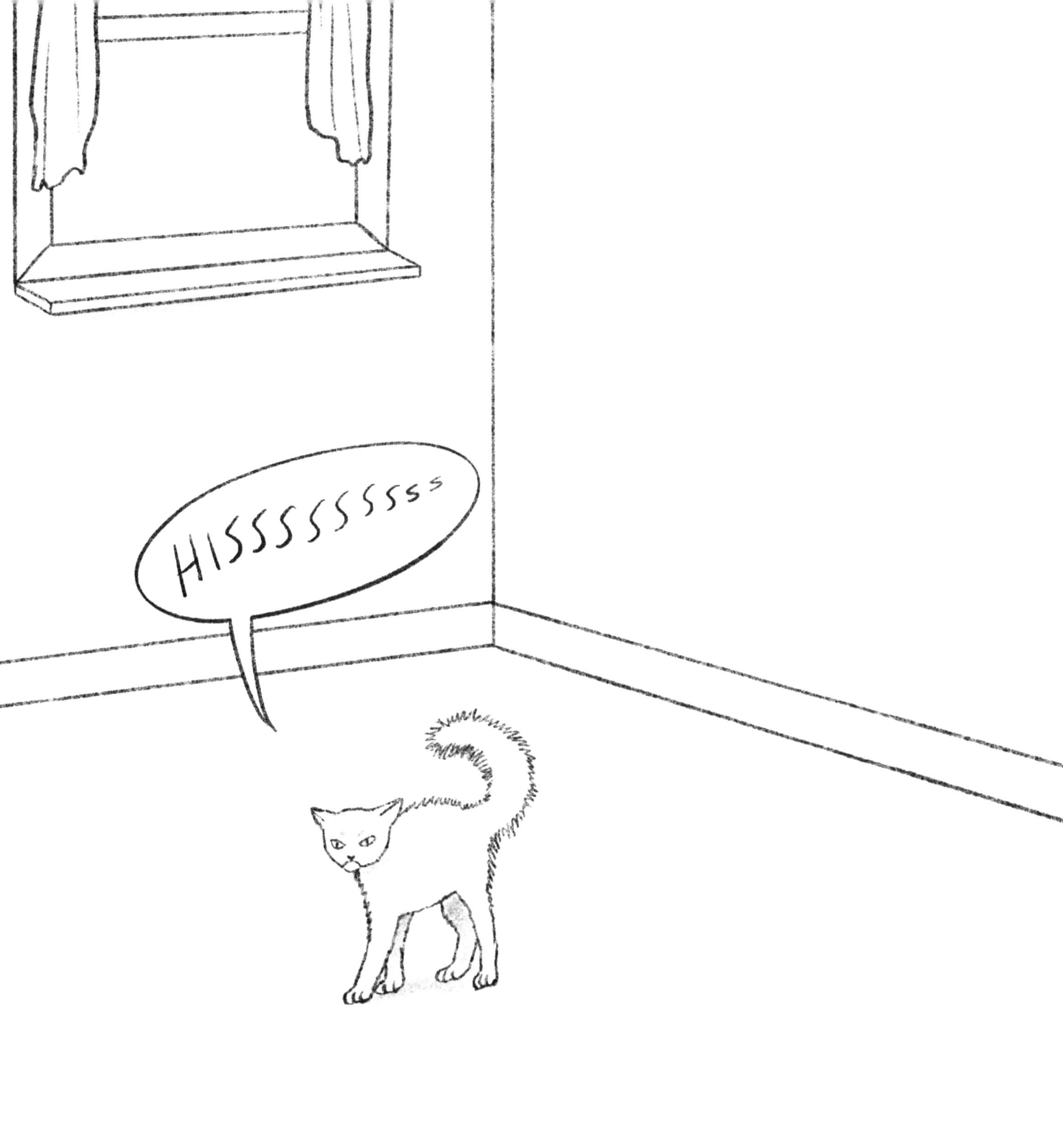
HISSSSSSSss

WHICH LADYBUG IS DIFFERENT?

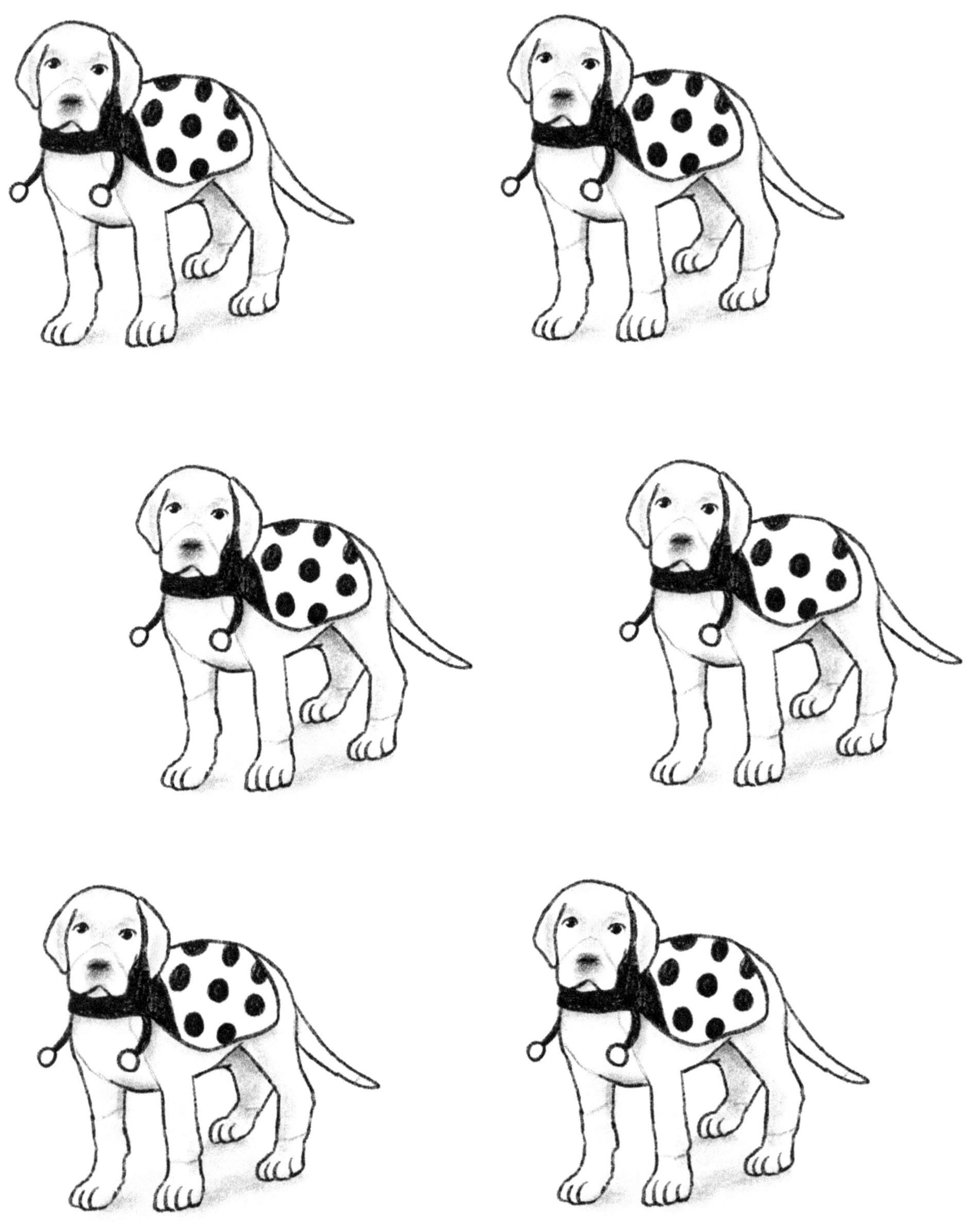

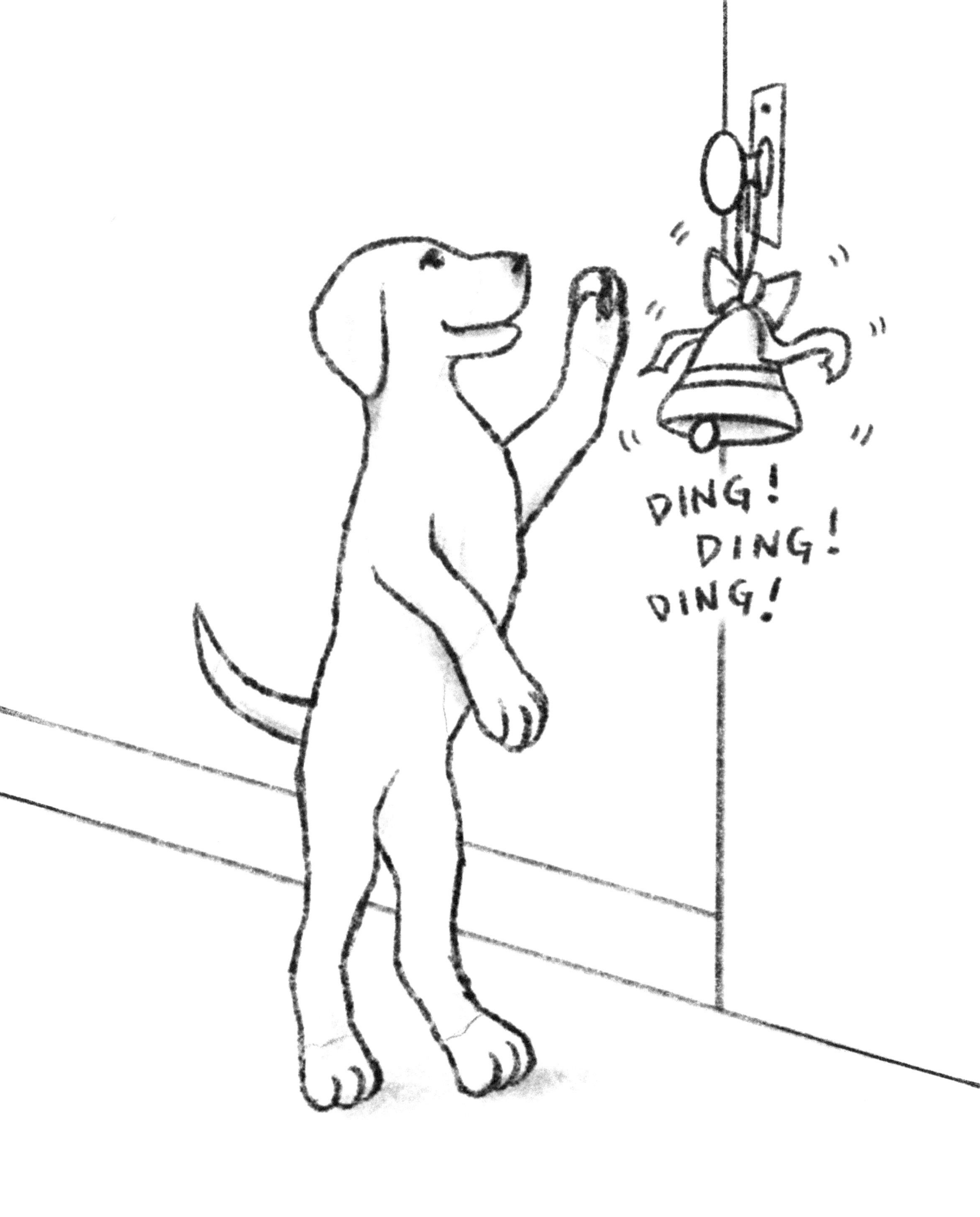
DING!
DING!
DING!

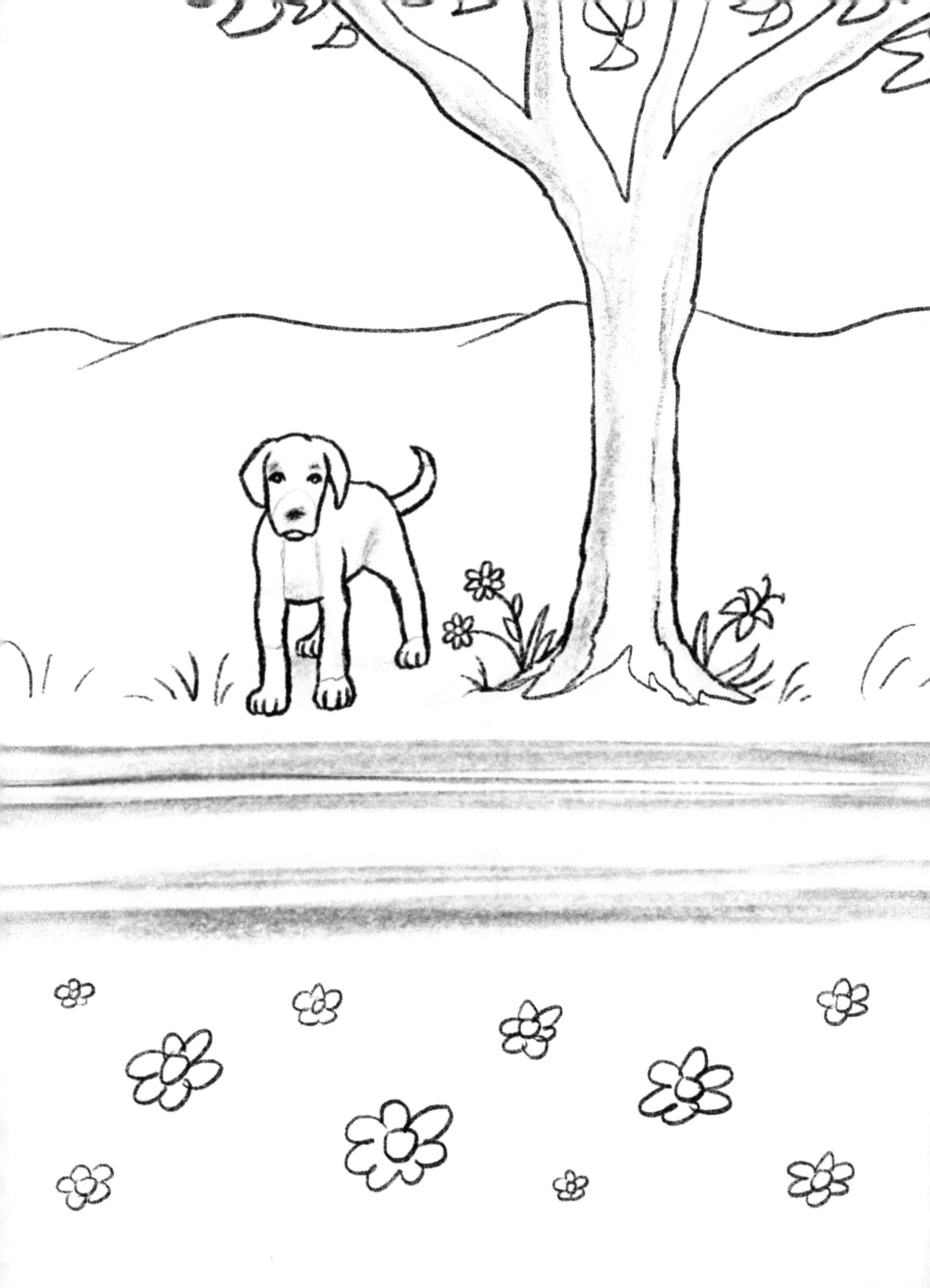

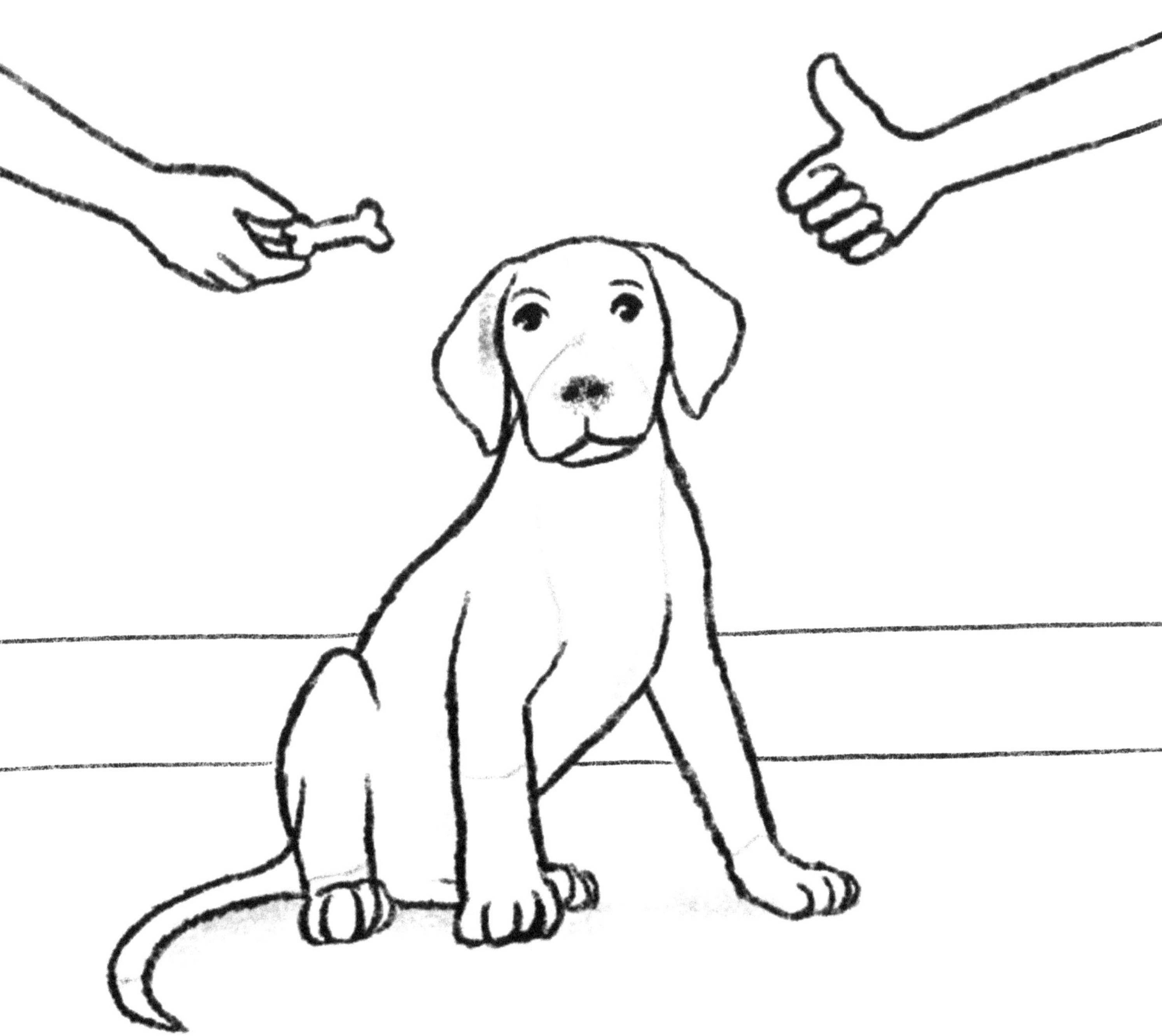

WHICH PUPPY

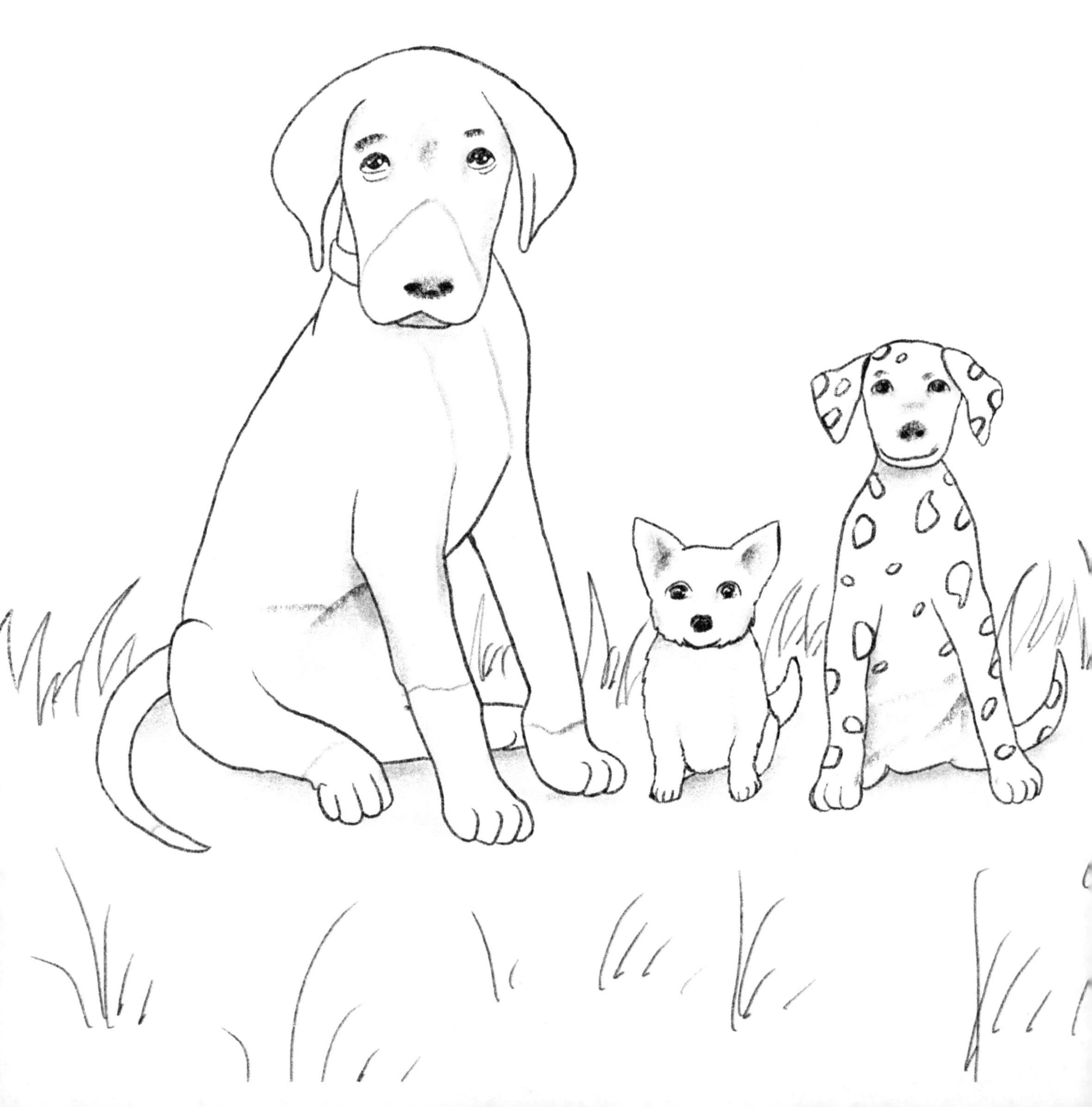

IS YOUR FAVORITE?

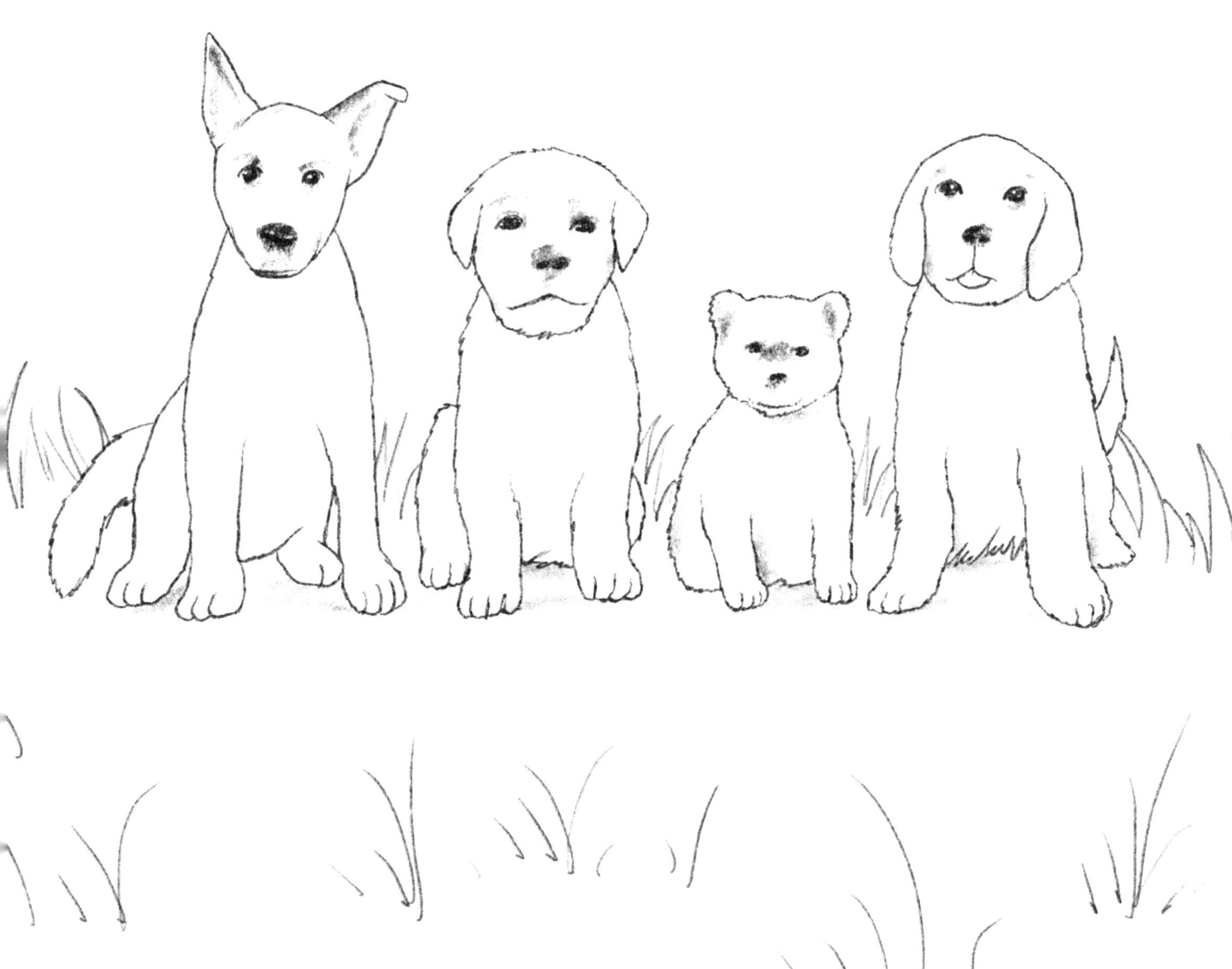

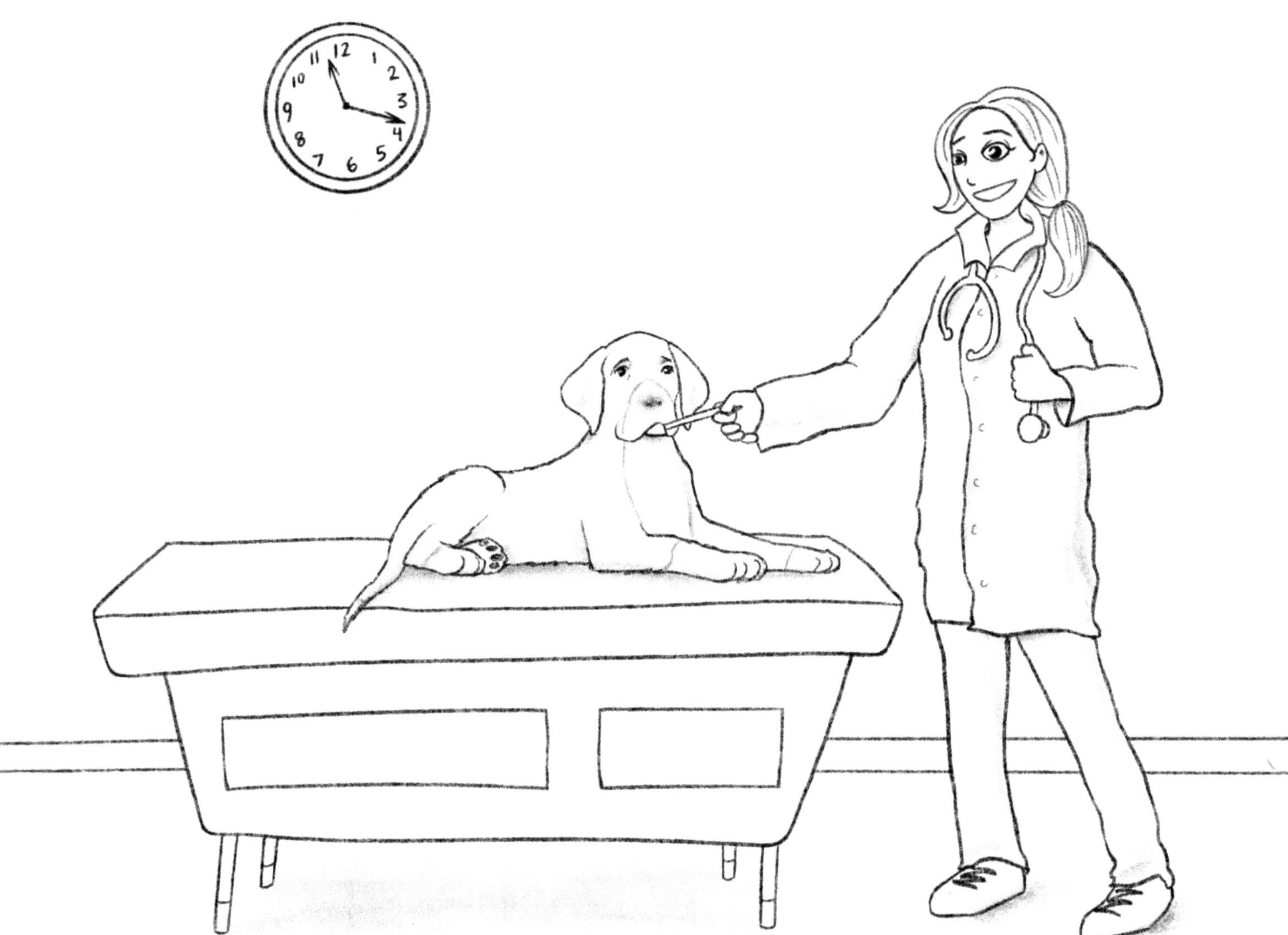

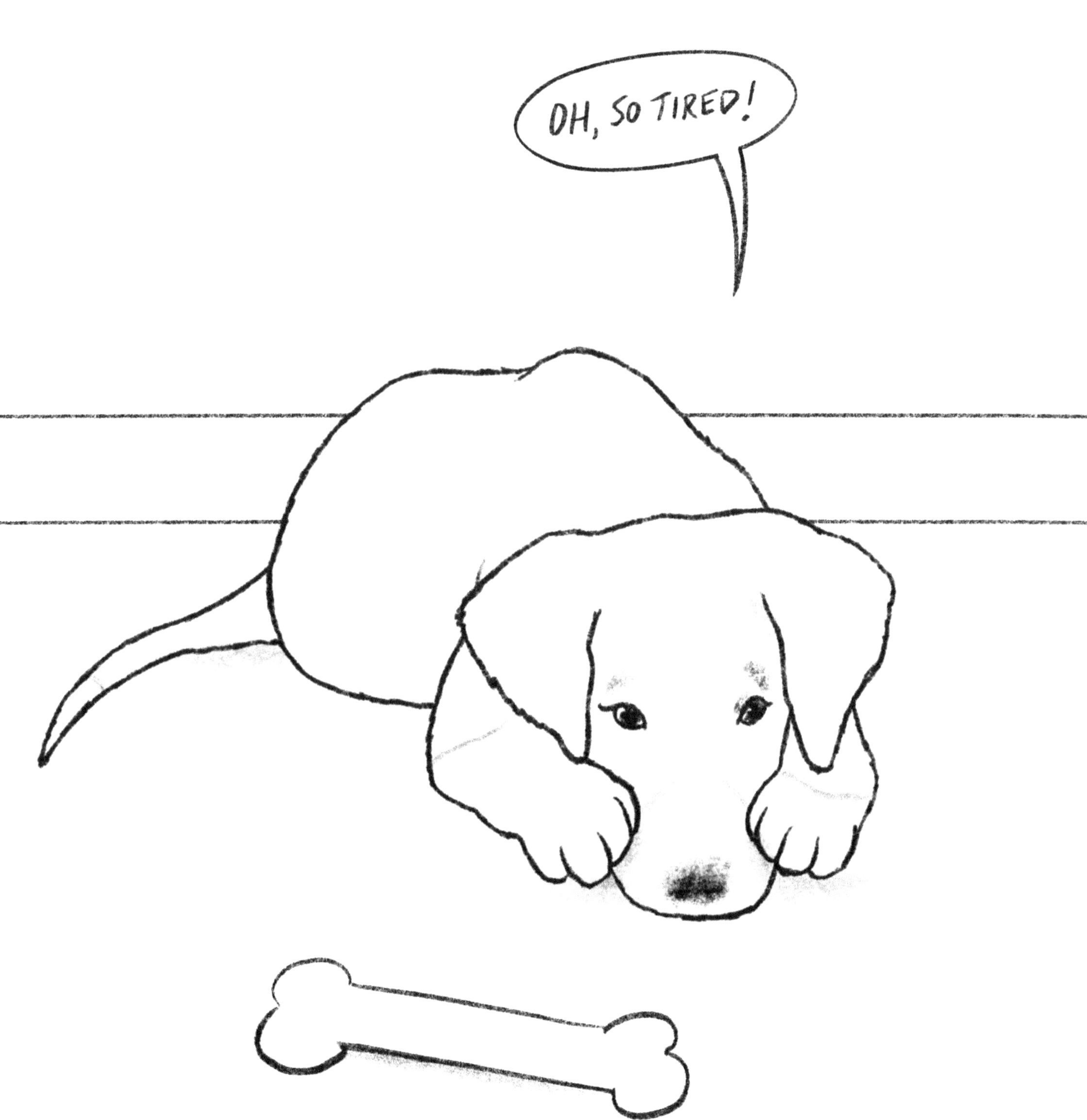
OH, SO TIRED!

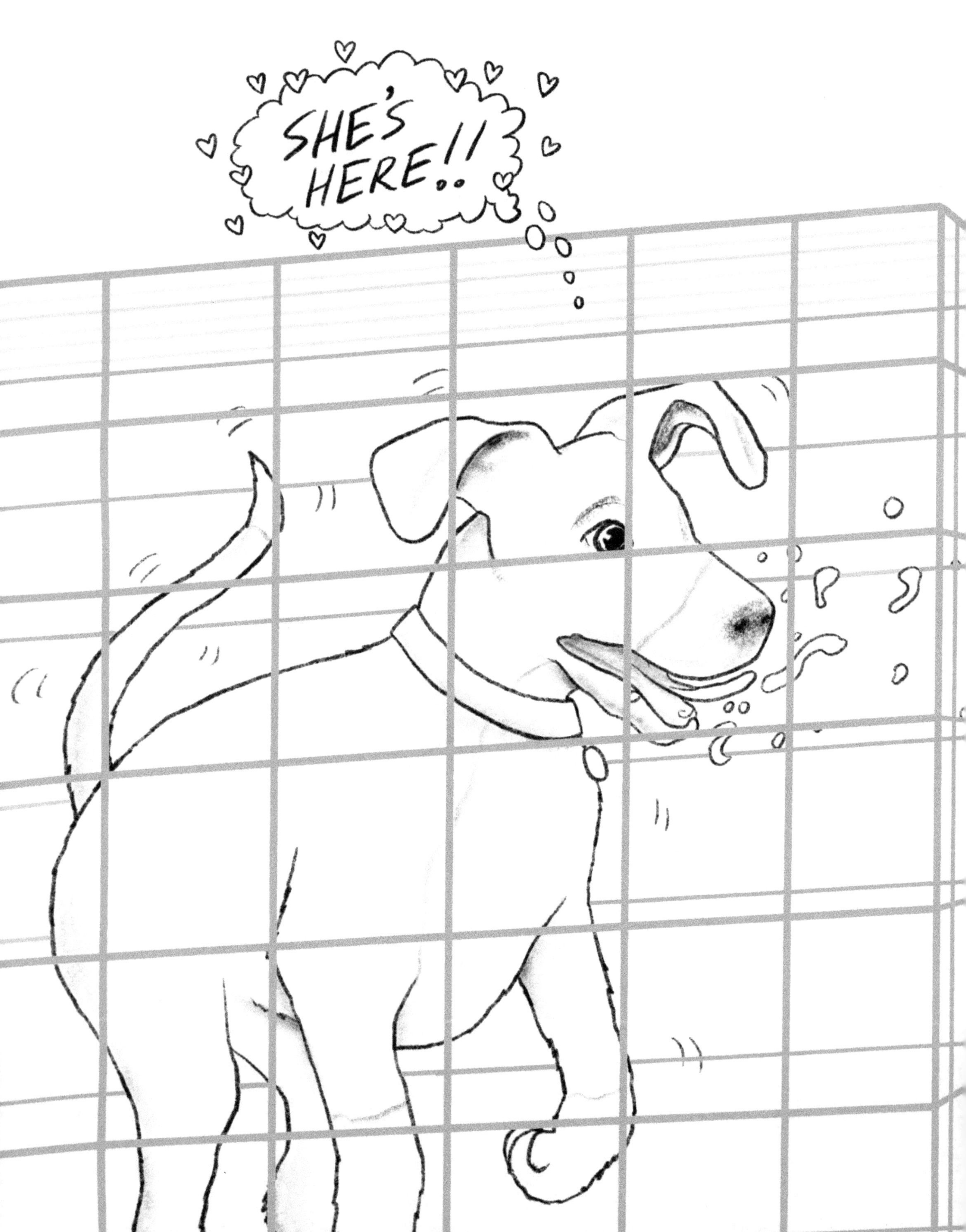
SHE'S HERE!!

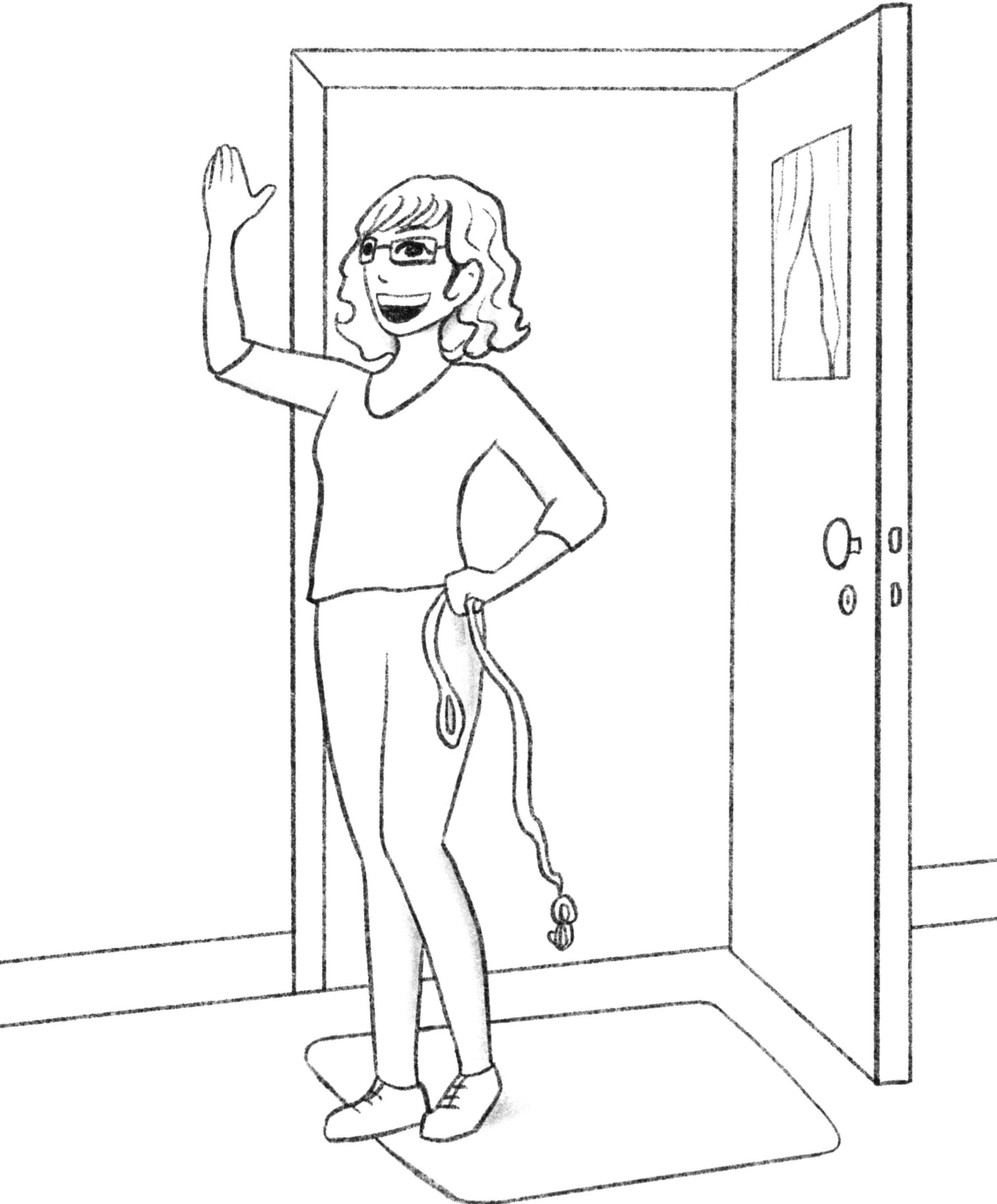

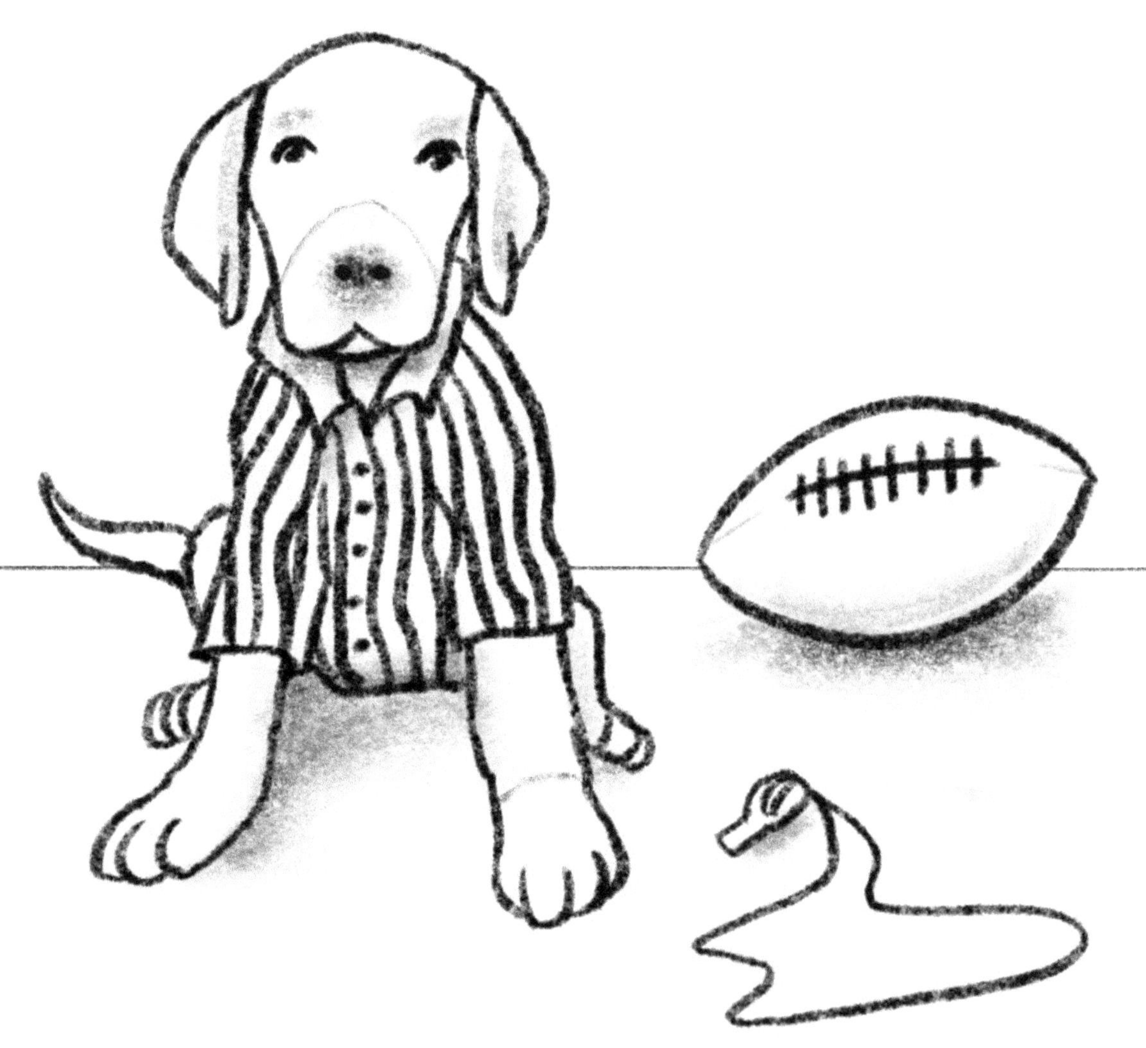

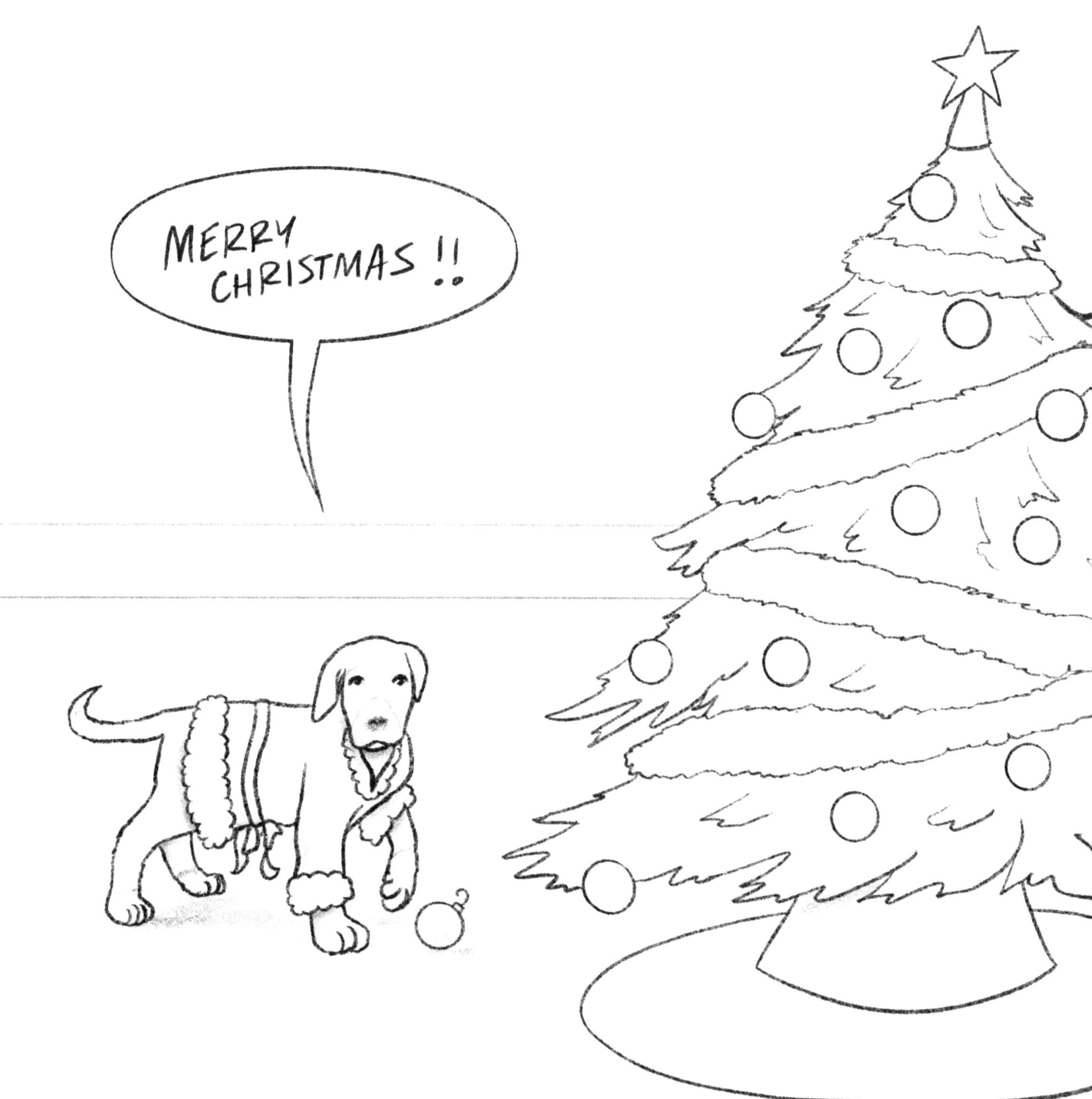
MERRY CHRISTMAS !!

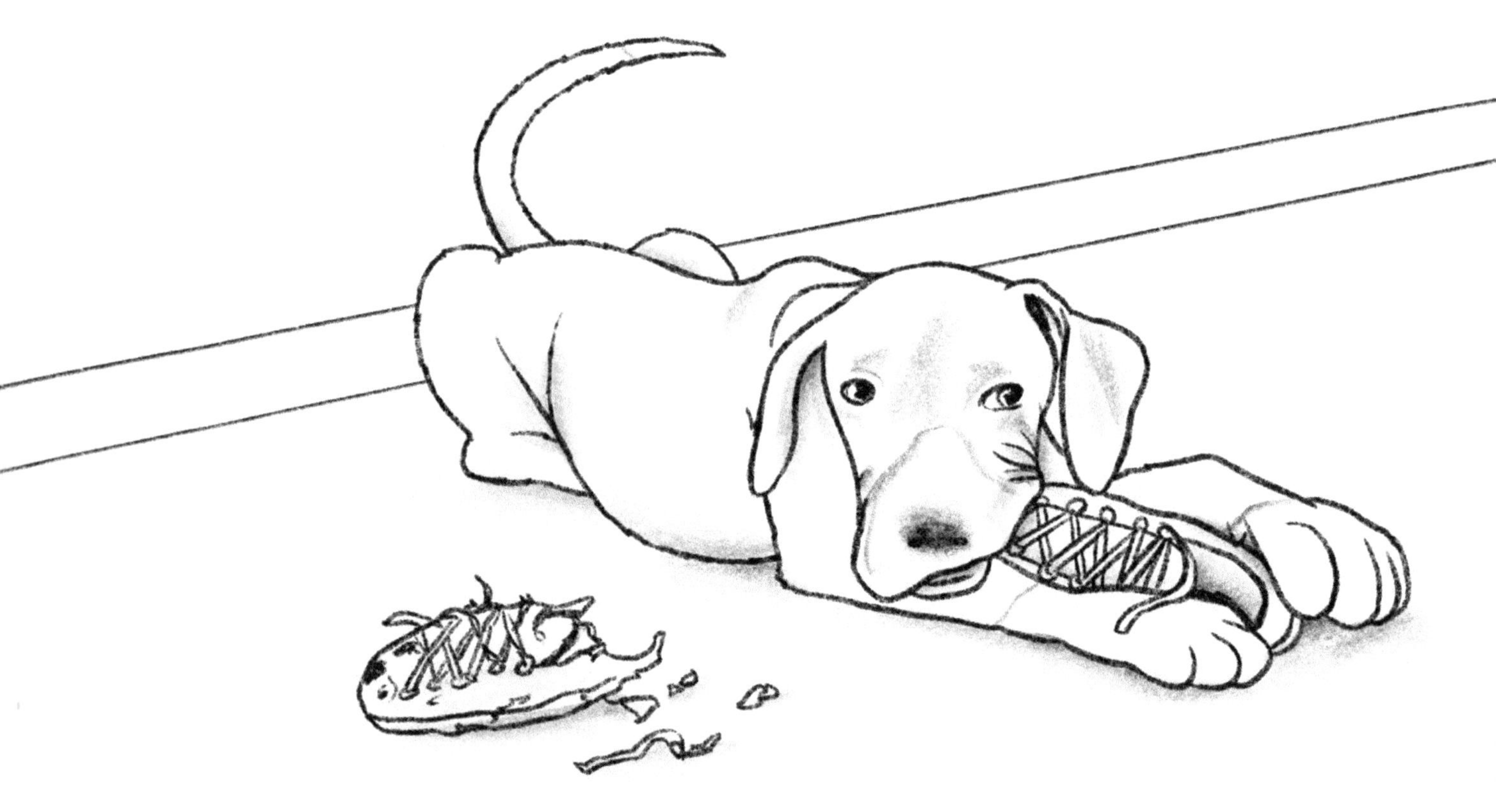

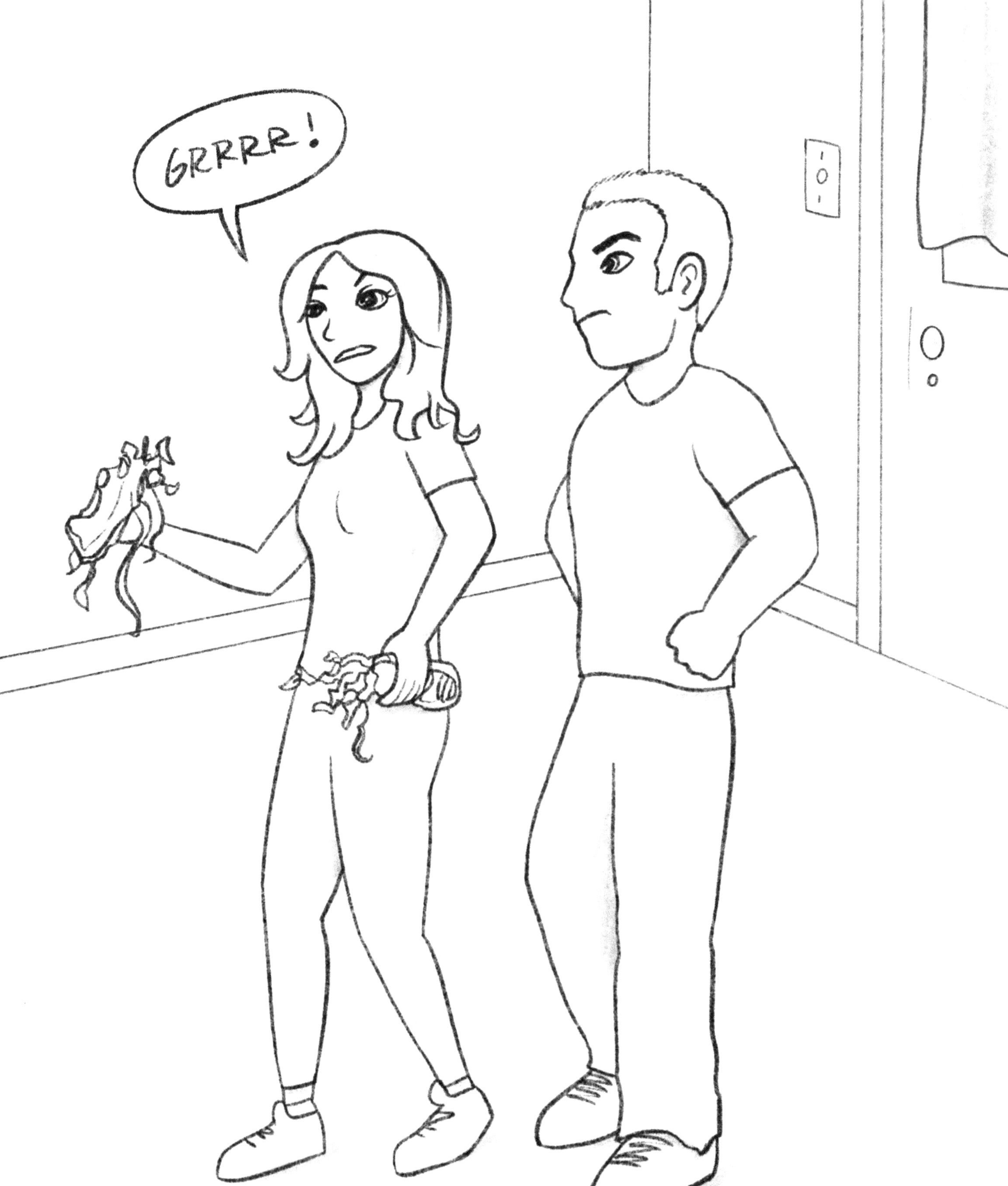
GRRRR!

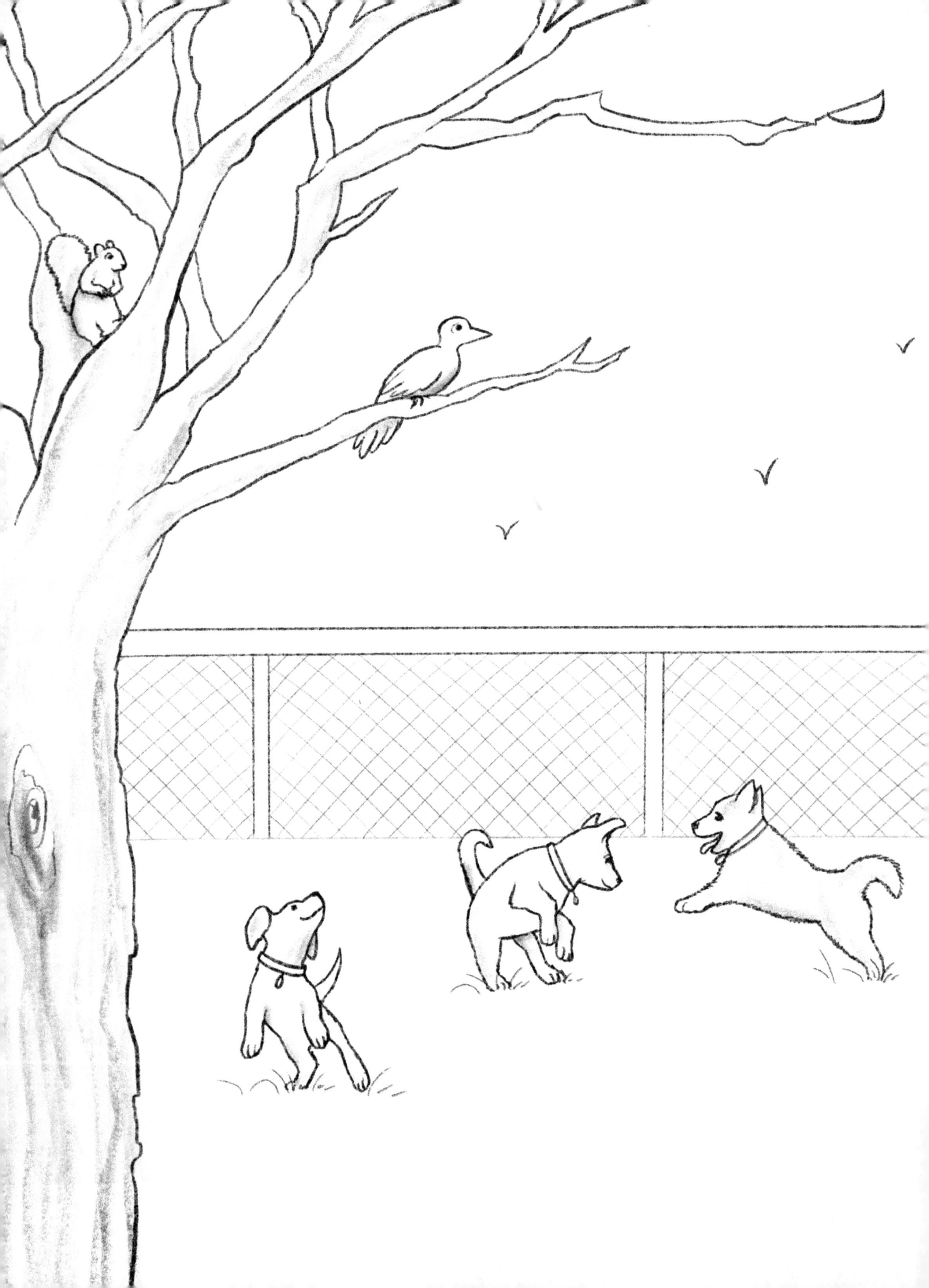

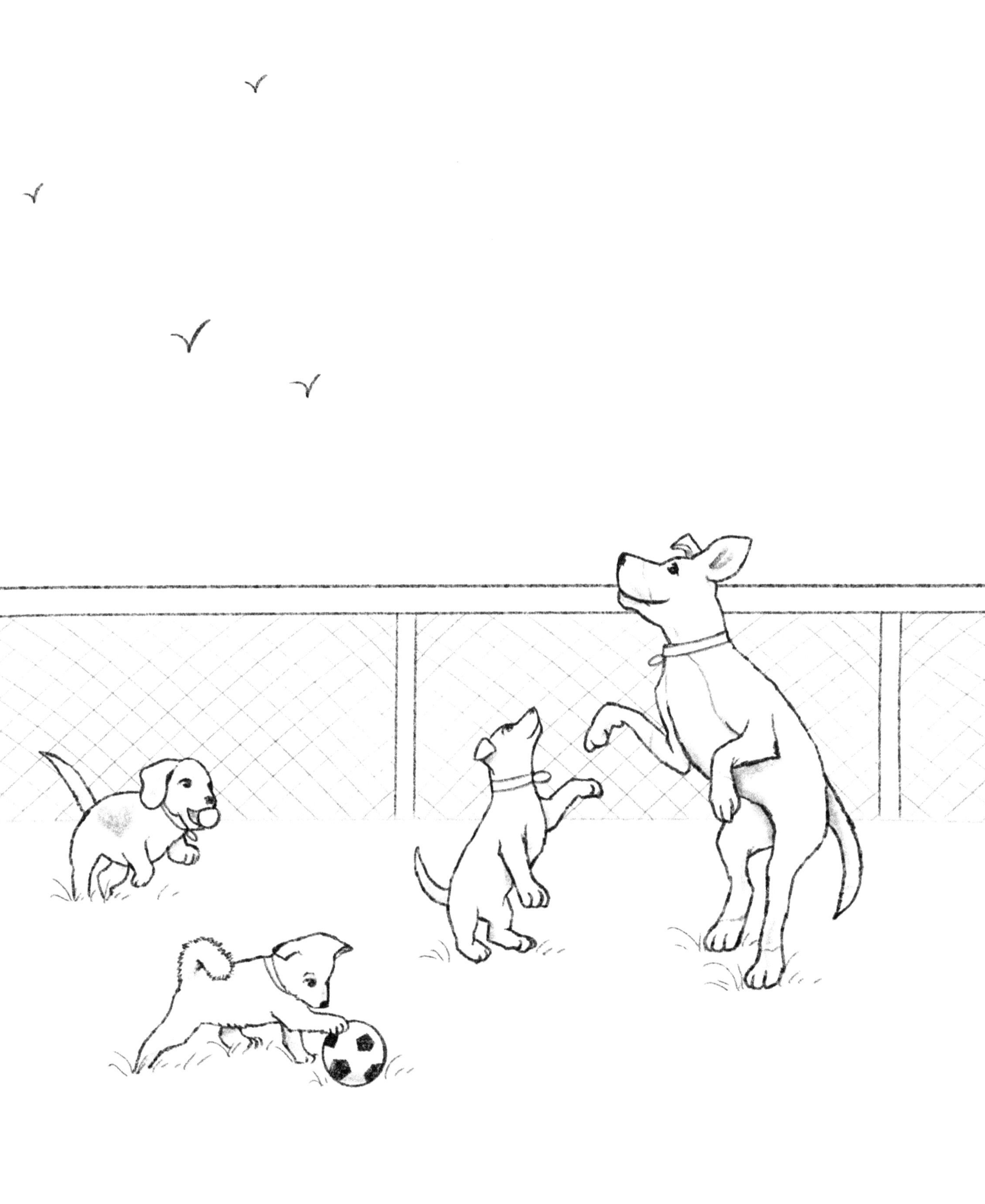

WEEEEE!!

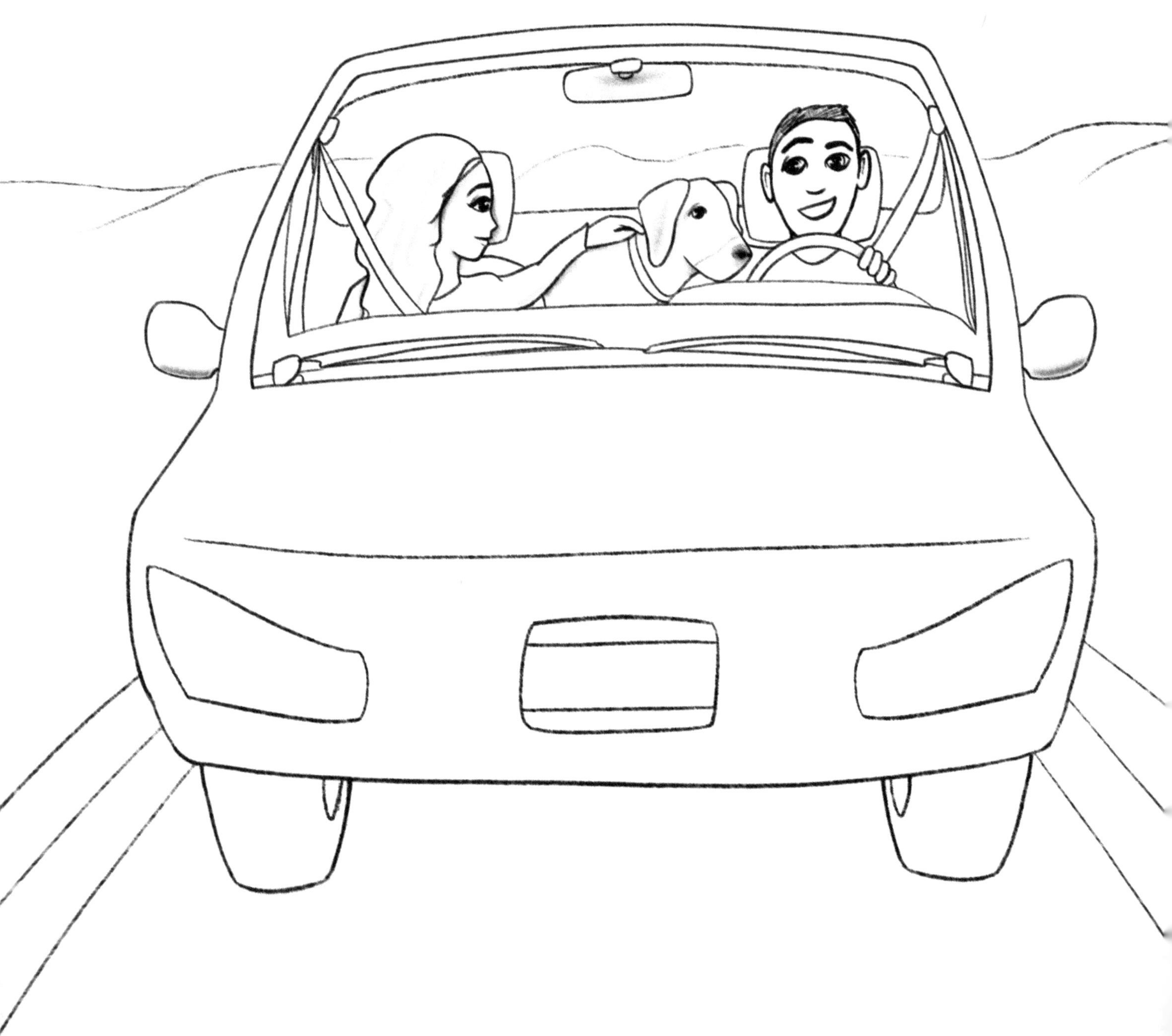

HELP FIND ABBEY'S FRIENDS FOR A PLAYDATE!

W	A	I	P	O	T	M	W	L
I	D	A	D	Y	R	N	S	A
K	S	B	A	U	S	H	U	M
L	S	B	S	L	T	J	N	P
P	R	E	C	I	O	U	S	T
J	L	Y	G	F	R	S	H	E
F	A	O	M	O	M	D	I	S
N	P	N	K	Q	B	O	N	D
M	U	K	D	W	X	J	E	N
U	I	D	A	R	Z	A	S	O
Y	S	H	D	E	E	N	H	L
D	O	C	T	O	R	W	V	M

ABBEY
ANDREW
DAD
DOCTOR

JAN
JEN
MOM
PJ

PRECIOUS
STORM
SUNSHINE

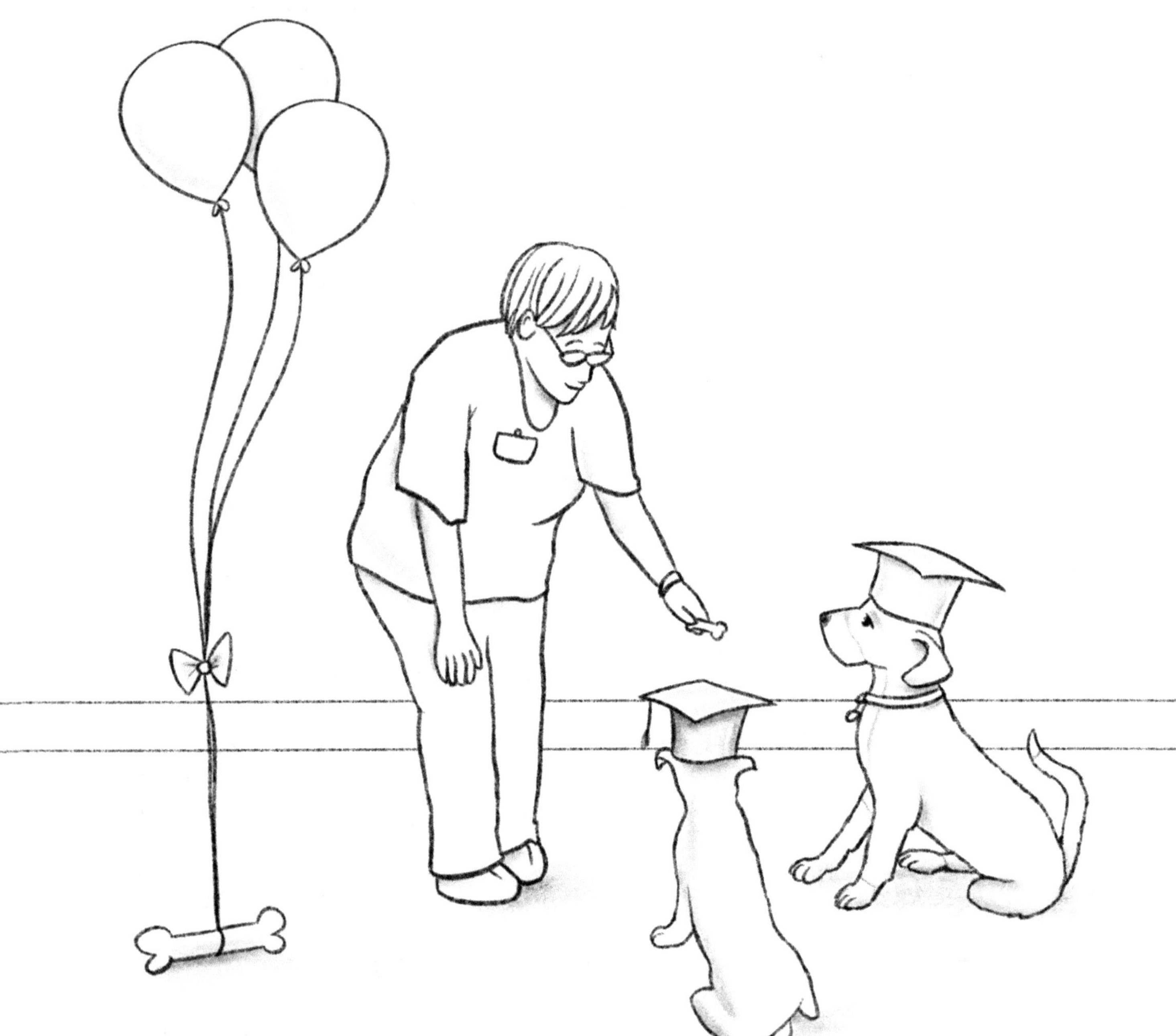

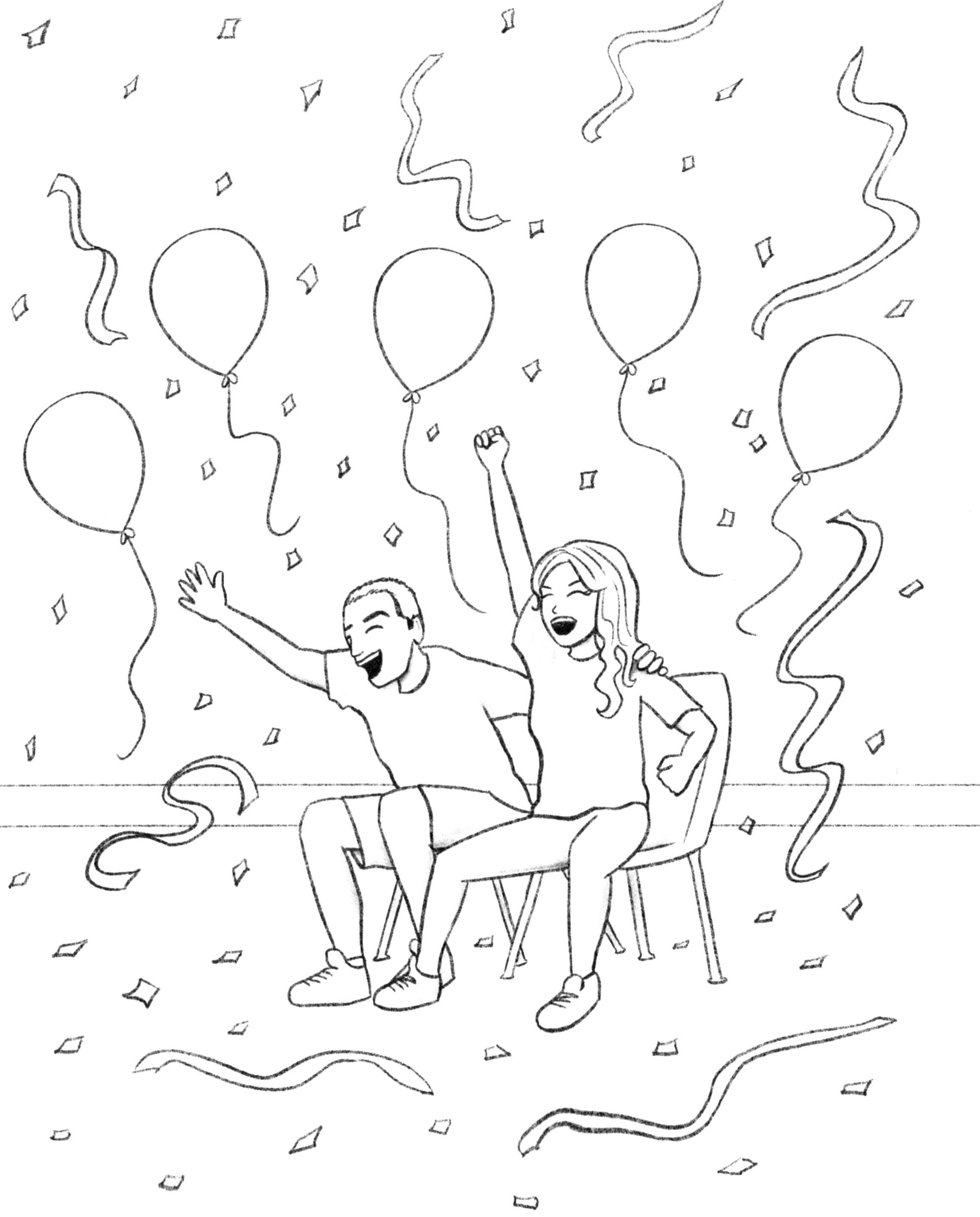

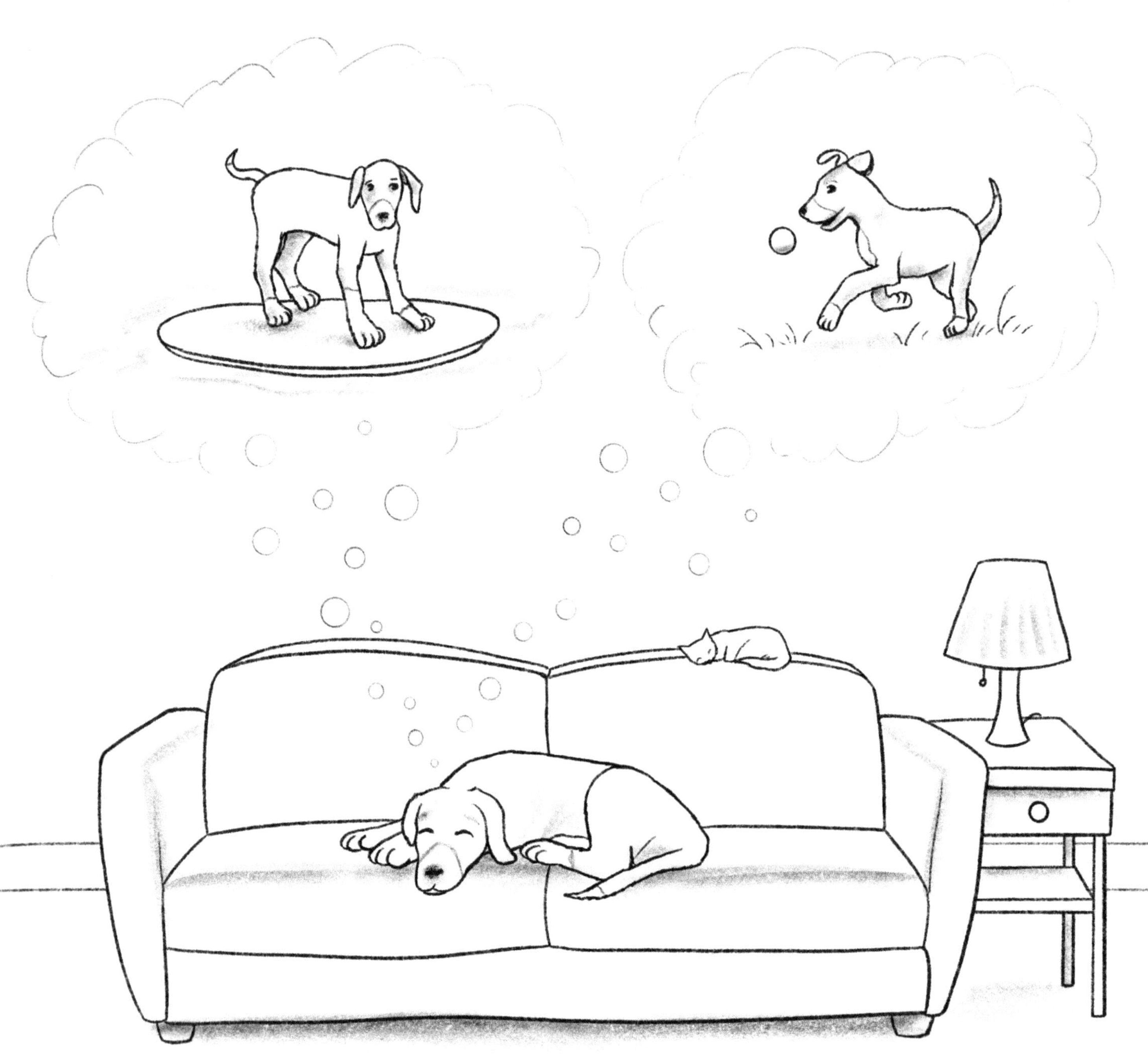

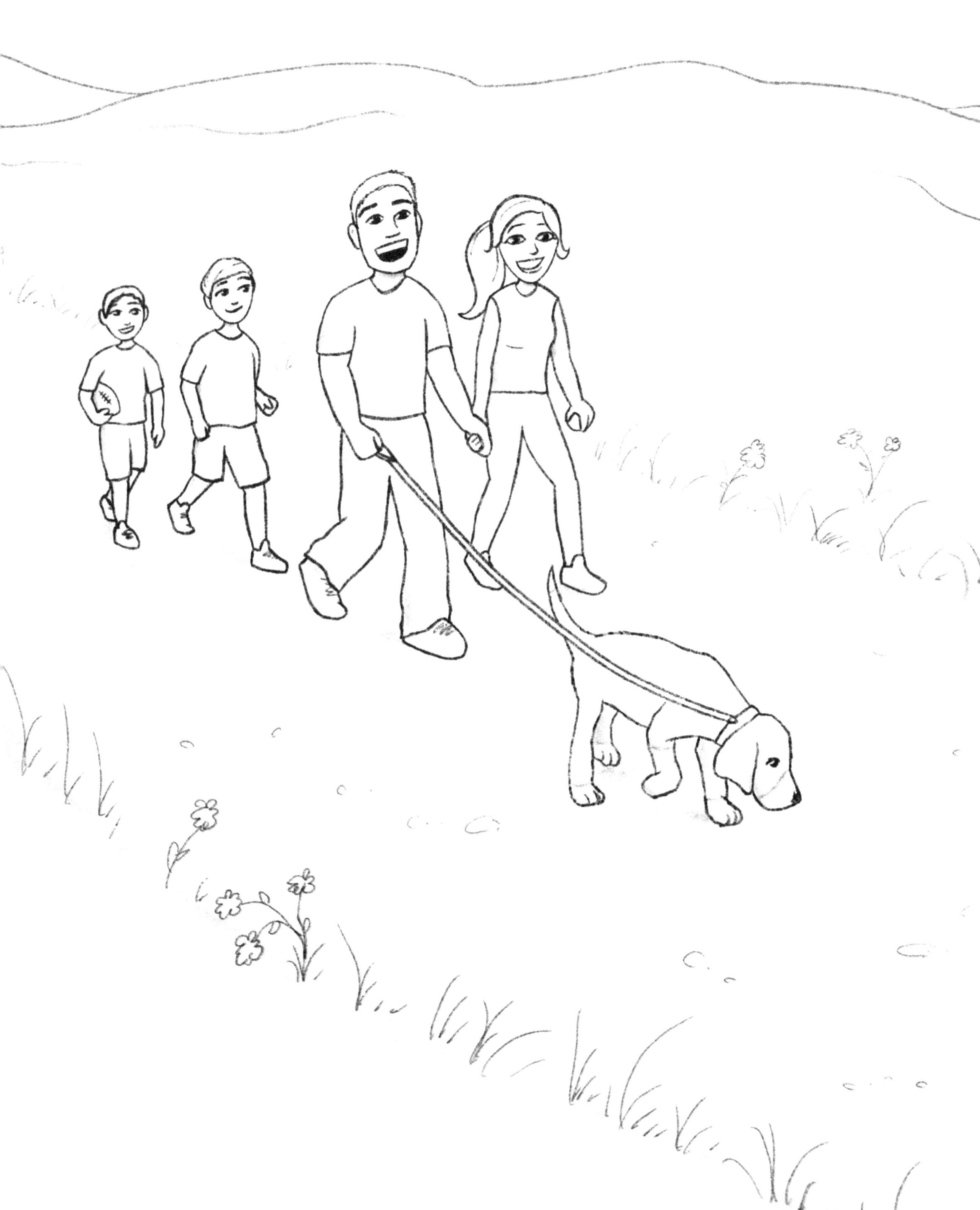

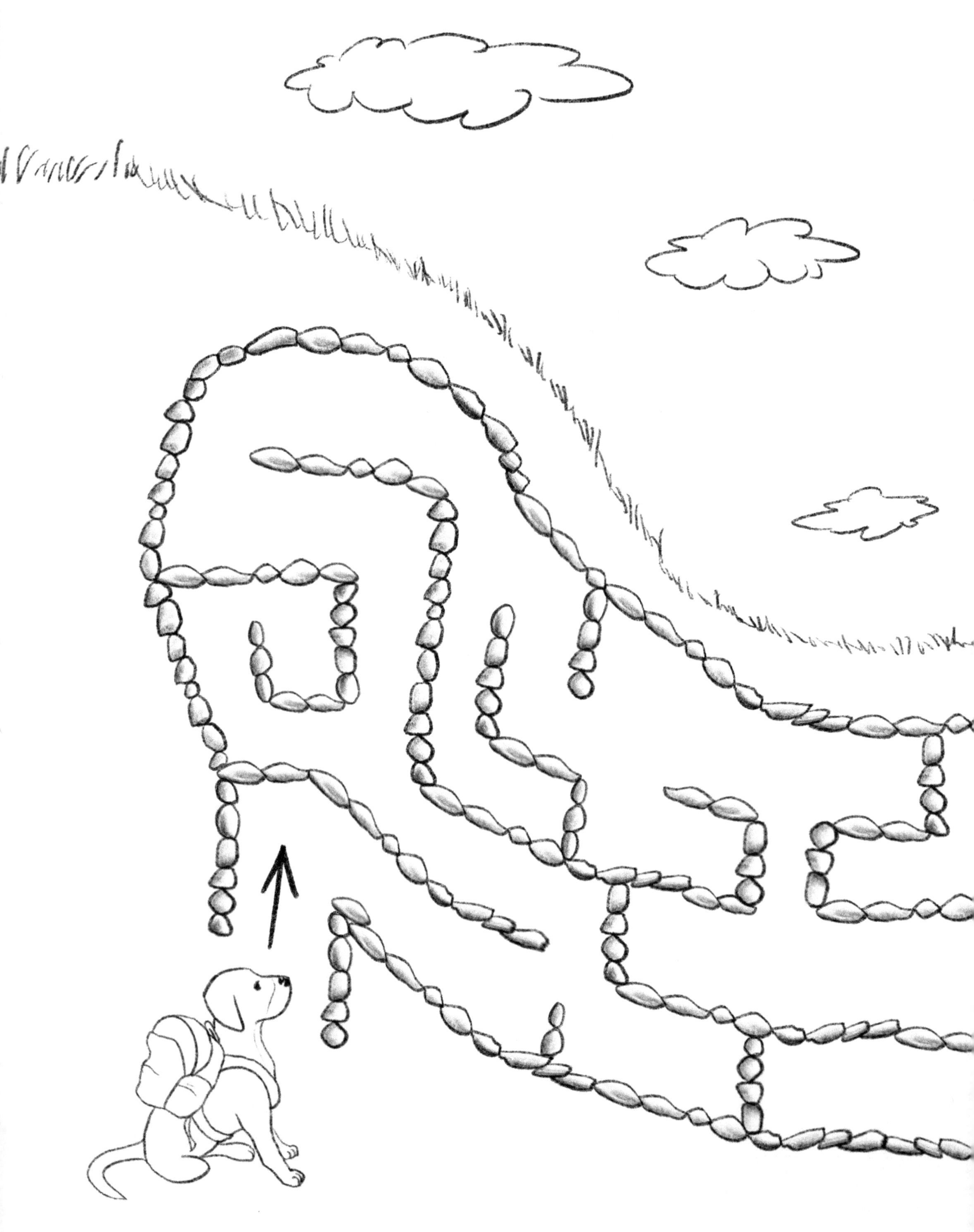

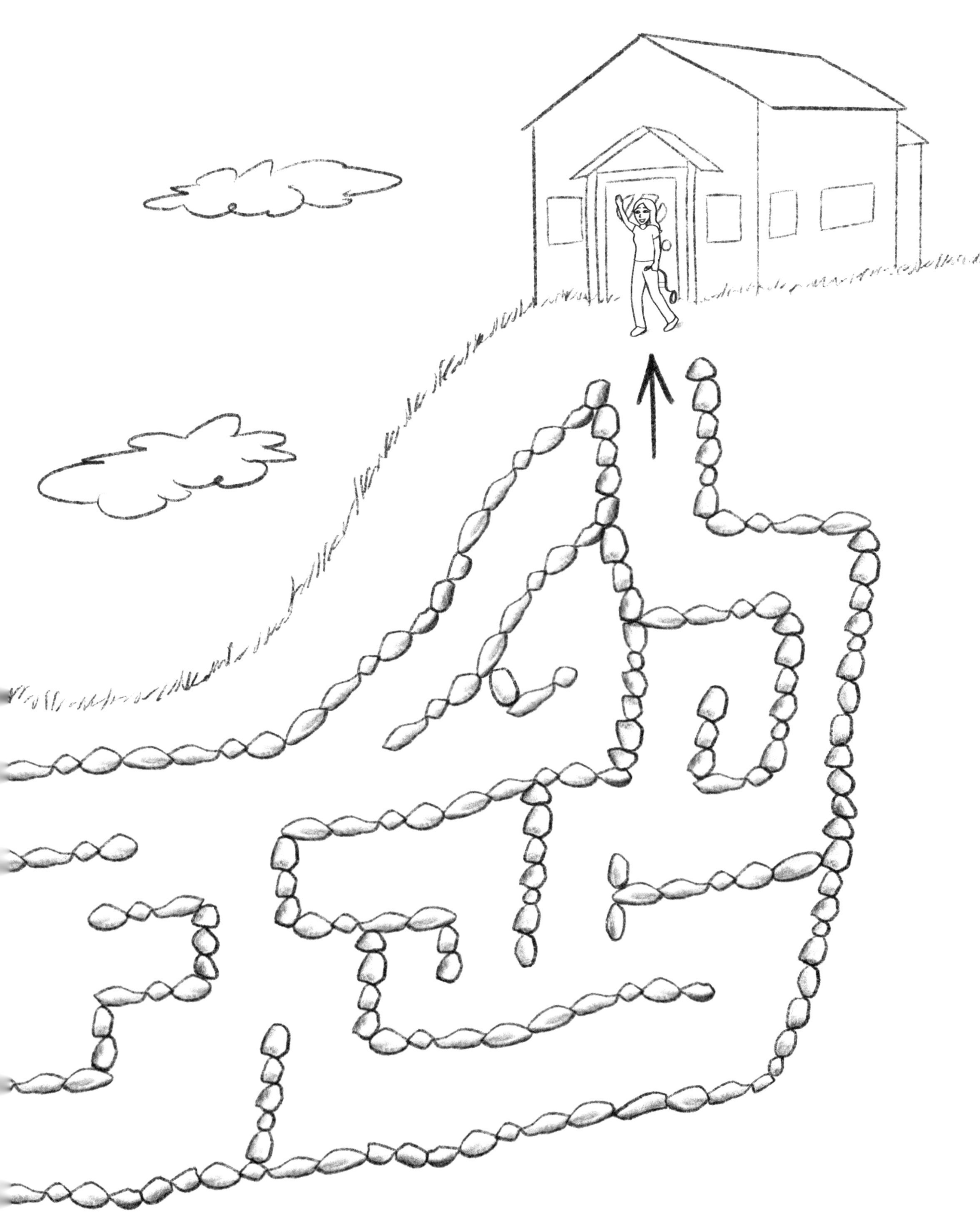

Published in 2023 by
Saratoga Springs Publishing, LLC
Saratoga Springs, NY 12866
www.SaratogaSpringsPublishing.com
Printed in the United States of America

ISBN-13: 978-1-955568-32-6
ISBN-10: 1-955568-32-4

Written by Diane Capogna
Illustrations by Anthony Richichi
Graphic Design by Emily Brooks
Publisher & Book design by Vicki Addesso Dodd

Saratoga Springs Publishing's books are available at a discount when purchased in quantity for promotions, fundraising and educational use. For additional information, book sales or events, contact us at
www.DianeCapogna.com or
dianecapogna@gmail.com

♥ I dedicate this book to my grandson Jordan Joseph Ross.
May your colors shine bright for all to see! ♥

www.ingramcontent.com/pod-product-compliance
Lightning Source LLC
LaVergne TN
LVHW081425110826
845149LV00010B/1872

* 9 7 8 1 9 5 5 5 6 8 3 2 6 *